THE INVESTOR'S GUIDEBOOK TO

EQUITIES

THE INVESTOR'S GUIDEBOOK TO

EQUITIES

Equity Pricing, Trading, and Investing

STUART R. VEALE

Prentice Hall Press

PRENTICE HALL PRESS
Published by the Penguin Group
Penguin Group (USA) LLC
375 Hudson Street, New York, New York 10014

USA • Canada • UK • Ireland • Australia • New Zealand • India • South Africa • China

penguin.com

A Penguin Random House Company

Library of Congress Cataloging-in-Publication Data

Veale, Stuart R.
The investor's guidebook to equities : equity pricing, trading, and investing / Stuart R. Veale.
pages   cm
Includes index.
ISBN 978-0-7352-0532-1 (pbk.)
1. Stocks.   2. Stocks—Prices.   3. Investment analysis.   I. Title.
HG4661.V43   2014
332.63'22—dc23   2013035847

First edition: January 2014

PRINTED IN THE UNITED STATES OF AMERICA

10   9   8   7   6   5   4   3   2   1

Most Prentice Hall Press books are available at special quantity discounts for bulk purchases for sales
promotions, premiums, fund-raising, or educational use. Special books, or book excerpts, can also
be created to fit specific needs. For details, write: Special.Markets@us.penguingroup.com.

This book is dedicated to the millions of investors who are trying to make sense of the stock market so they can obtain a safe and secure retirement for themselves and their families. This is no easy task. Some estimates predict fewer than 15% of Americans will accumulate enough assets to enjoy a safe and secure retirement. While investing in stocks is challenging, it is often an investor's best chance of obtaining the wealth and income they need to retire.

ACKNOWLEDGMENTS

The author would like to thank William Addis who helped write and update the chapter on equity trading. As always, the author would like to thank Jeanette Shaw and her amazing team at Penguin. Working under incredibly short deadlines, they turned my notes into the attractive finished product you have in your hands.

CONTENTS

FOREWORD

I finished the second edition of my book on investing called *Stocks, Bonds, Options, Futures* (*SBOF*) in 2001. Here we are 12 years later. While the second edition was still selling well, it was also overdue for an update. Over the last 12 years, much has changed in the way stocks and bonds were priced, traded, analyzed, packaged, and marketed. Specialists on the New York Stock Exchange were replaced with designated market makers. The volume of trades executed on the dark pools soared. Derivatives on rainfall and wind had become hot products. Twenty-four-hour trading became a reality. The variety of exotic options exploded. Exchange-traded funds became the fastest growing financial product in history, etc.

I started out to write the third edition of *SBOF*, but it quickly became clear the industry had become too broad and too complex to comfortably fit in one text. Therefore, after discussing it with my publisher and readers, I made the decision to break the book into four manageable volumes:

- *The Investor's Guidebook to Derivatives*
- *The Investor's Guidebook to Alternative Investments*

- *The Investor's Guidebook to Fixed Income Investments*
- *The Investor's Guidebook to Equities*

My hope is that by expanding the book into four volumes, I'll be able to make them more comprehensive, include more examples, and make the books more useful to my readers. While I made every effort to proof the text, there will undoubtedly be errors for which I assume full responsibility. It is my intent to update these volumes frequently, and therefore, I welcome my readers' suggestions on which topics should be added, expanded, and omitted in future editions. Please email your questions, critiques, and comments to stu@invest-perform.com. I hope to answer every email I receive.

This book was prepared from sources believed to be reliable but which are not guaranteed. The research analyst who is primarily responsible for this research and whose name is listed on the front cover certifies that: (1) All of the views expressed in this research accurately reflect my personal views about any and all of the subject securities or issuers; and (2) no part of any of my compensation was, is, or will be directly or indirectly related to the specific recommendations or views expressed herein. Opinions and estimates constitute my judgment as of this writing and are subject to change without notice. Past performance is not indicative of future results. This material is not intended as an offer or solicitation for the purchase or sale of any financial instrument. Securities, financial instruments, or strategies mentioned herein may not be suitable for all investors. The opinions and recommendations herein do not take into account individual client circumstances, objectives, or needs, and are not intended as recommendations of particular securities, financial instruments, or strategies to particular clients. The reader must make independent decisions regarding any securities or financial instruments mentioned herein.

INTRODUCTION

One hundred years ago stocks were primarily owned by the very wealthy. Today, the majority of adults in the United States own stock either directly—or indirectly through their IRAs, 401(k) plans, and company pension plans. The US equity market is one of the most important tools for building wealth. It has allowed business owners to raise billions of dollars of capital to start and grow businesses. Over the last 70 years, it has allowed the creation of millions of jobs and rewarded investors with average returns well above those available from bank deposits or bonds.

Investing in stocks is one of the three primary drivers behind people becoming millionaires—the other two being starting a business and investing in real estate. Today's stock market has the highest liquidity, lowest transaction charges, widest range of powerful stock selection and management tools, and greatest variety of investment alternatives. This book provides investors with the essential background information they need to begin their study of the stock market. While this book provides a foundation of knowledge, studying the stock market is a lifelong undertaking.

Some of the chapters are primarily targeted at investors, while others are targeted primarily at analysts. As always, the hard part of writing a book like this is what to leave out. I intentionally left out data on market size, trading volumes, and the like. This data is readily available on the web and is constantly changing. I instead tried to focus on the concepts that will help investors select and implement an appropriate strategy.

CHAPTER ONE

Introduction to Stocks

WHAT ARE STOCKS?

Stocks are certificates that represent an ownership interest in a company. If a company has issued 100 shares of stock and you own one, you own a 1/100 interest (1%) in the company. If you own all 100 shares, then you own the entire company. If a company has issued 168,250,000 shares of stock and you own 1,250 of them, you own a 1,250/168,250,000 = 0.0007429421% interest in the company. As a shareholder you enjoy many of the advantages and the disadvantages of being a company owner.

WHAT ARE THE ADVANTAGES OF INVESTING IN STOCKS?

The first advantage of owning a company (and the advantage of greatest interest for investors) is an almost unlimited opportunity for profits. A relatively small investment in the right company at the right time can grow to be millions or even tens of millions of dollars. For example, $10,000 invested in each of the companies listed next would have grown to the following staggering sums (exclusive of dividend reinvestment):

Apple	$1.78 (1982) to $675 (2012)	$3,792,135
Microsoft	$0.10 (1987) to $59.97 (1999)	$5,997,000
Cisco	$0.07 (1991) to $82 (2000)	$11,714,286
Walmart	$0.02 (1974) to $72 (1999)	$36,000,000
Berkshire	$18.50 (1974) to $151,650 (2007)	$81,972,973

The next advantage of investing in stocks is that they offer a limited downside. If you buy $20k worth of stock, the most you can lose is 100% of your money. While losing 100% is not a good outcome, it is possible with other investments (certain derivatives and starting your own business) to lose a multiple of your original investment.

Owning stock is a tax-advantaged investment. Stocks have several tax advantages associated with them. First, for stocks that don't pay dividends, investors only pay taxes on their gains when they sell. Paying taxes only at the end of the investment instead of each year allows account value to grow much faster. Consider an account where you start with $10K and earn 10% a year. In one case, you are taxed each year on the gains at 50% (netting 5%); in the other, you are only taxed at 50% at the end of 30 years:

- Taxed each year: $10,000 \times (1.05)^{30} = \$43,219$ ending balance, for a gain of $33,219
- Taxed at end of investment: $10,000 \times (1.10)^{30} = \$174,494$ ending balance. $10,000 starting value: gain of $164,494 \times .5$ taxes $= \$82,247$ after-tax + $10,000 initial value = $92,247 ending balance—almost three times as much!

Second, when your gains are taxed, they are often taxed at a rate that is lower than the ordinary tax rate—that is, the capital gains rate. As the time of writing, this was 20% for high net worth investors. Third, since you decide when to sell, you can sell in years when your tax rate is lower—i.e., after you retire.

When you own stock, you also gain:

- **Voting rights for members of the board of directors**—The board of directors is the ultimate power within a company. The board represents the owners. Most common stock provides one vote per share for each seat on the board of directors. Each seat comes up for election every 1 to 3 years. If you want your company to expand in China, you can vote for board candidates who want to expand in China. If you want your company to buy its suppliers, you can vote for board candidates who want to buy the company's suppliers. If you want the company to raise its dividend payments, you can vote for board candidates that want to raise dividends. As with any democracy, majority rules. (Beware—there are companies out there that have multiple classes of common stock and some of those classes have no voting rights.)

- **The ability to quickly change allocation and focus**—An often overlooked advantage of investing in common stock is that investors can quickly change focus. For example, suppose for whatever reason you think now is a great time to be in the airline business. You can either start an airline company or simply invest in United, Delta, Japan Airlines, and the like. Either way, if your underlying assumption that "now is a good time to be in the airline business" is correct, either approach will be successful. However, in 4 years if it is no longer a good time to be in the airline business but is instead a good time to be in the oil business, it is a lot easier to sell your airline stocks and buy oil stocks than to transition an airline company into an oil company.

- **Fun**—Buying stocks is fun. It is an adult intellectual sport. Your ability to select which stocks to buy (or sell) and when to buy (or sell) them is pitted against every other investor in the world. To the extent you out-think and out-act your opponents, you win. Stocks are fun to research, to talk about, and even fun to complain about when they don't cooperate.

- **A wide range of reward/risk trade-offs**—There are stocks for investors who have a high tolerance for risk and a potentially very high reward. For example, companies that are pursuing revolutionary new technologies or are prospecting for gold or oil offer both high risk and high potential reward. There are also stocks that have a very low level of risk and are suitable for very conservative investors such as utility stocks, cable companies, and water companies. Naturally these stocks offer a much lower potential reward.

- **The ability to manage inflation risk**—During inflationary times companies can usually increase their prices and profits in line with inflation. This provides some protection against inflation that other investments, such as bonds, do not offer.

WHAT ARE THE DISADVANTAGES OF OWNING STOCK?

Owning stocks also has some powerful disadvantages. Before investing in stocks, every investor should carefully consider these disadvantages:

- **Owners are the last to get paid**—Stockholders, as owners, get paid after employees, landlords, taxes, vendors, bondholders, and so forth. Sometimes, by the time everyone else is paid, there's nothing left for the owner!

- **Triple price sensitivity**—The price of a stock depends not only on the company's individual success, but also on whether the market as a whole is rising or falling and whether the currency in which the stock is denominated is rising or falling. It is frustrating as a shareholder to select a great company and have its success negated by a bad market environment and/or an adverse currency move. To maximize the return, you need to select a great company and buy it in a rising market in a currency that is either your reference currency or will strengthen against your currency!

- **Fraud**—The usefulness of any analysis of a company's financial results is going to be limited by the accuracy of those financials. If the financial statements are fraudulent, then any analysis based on them is a complete waste of time.

- **Learning curve**—Successfully investing in stocks requires coming up a learning curve. One that can take a lifetime. It is important to approach investing seriously.

How Is Stock Created?

Only a corporation can issue stock. A corporation is a business that, in the eyes of the law, is a separate legal entity from the people that own and/or work for the company (unlike sole proprietorships and partnerships). In the United States, corporations come in two forms: Subchapter S and Subchapter C.

- **A Subchapter S Corporation**—This is a limited corporation in that it is only allowed to have a maximum of 75 shareholders and is, therefore, suitable only for small and midsize businesses.

- **A Subchapter C Corporation**—This is a fully separate legal entity. The advantage this offers is that shareholders who are not part of senior management are not liable for any losses or damages done by the companies they own. For example, when Enron went bankrupt, it left behind almost $8 billion in unpaid bills, wages, pensions, taxes, rent, and the like, and the shareholders were not liable for any of it. The disadvantage of C corporations is that, as a separate legal entity, they are taxed on their profits before they distribute them to their owners. Since the distributions are then taxed again, distributions are subject to double taxation. All public companies are C corporations.

How Is a Corporation Created?

A corporation is created by filing the requisite application form with the Secretary of State of any one of the fifty states. Most states allow filing "online." You can select *any* state you want. The state in which the corporation is created does not have to be the one in which you live, are headquartered, do business, or a state in which you have operations. You may have to maintain a minimal presence in the state consisting of a phone and a mailbox. However, once you select a state, your corporation has to follow that state's rules and regulations for operating your business and maintaining the corporation. Some of the many decisions you may have to make when you incorporate include:

- What will be the name of the company? You have to be careful to select a name that does not violate anyone else's copyright or trademark. Even if your name is Ford, you can't start a car company named Ford. You may want to select a name you can trademark yourself in order to build brand equity.

- What is your company's fiscal year? It can end on any date you choose. It is usually better to not pick Dec 31 or April 15 since that's when accountants are the busiest.
- How many people will you put on your board of directors and how often will your board meet? The board of directors is the ultimate power within the corporation. For a small company where you own all the stock, you may be the only board member. It is the board that hires the company's managers, sets the company's policy and strategic direction, and approves all major expenditures.
- Who will be the company's officers? At a minimum you'll need a president, secretary, and treasurer. They can all be the same person—you—or each position can be filled by a separate person. Each officer will have certain legal responsibilities depending on the state in which you incorporate.
- How many outside directors vs. inside directors to have on the board. An inside director is someone who works for, or provides services to, a company. For example, a family-owned and -run business might have the CEO (who is a family member), the company treasurer (who is a family member), a lawyer (from the firm the company uses for legal work), and an accountant (from the firm's accounting firm) on its board. All would be inside directors. The fear is that inside directors might not disagree with the CEO even if the CEO suggests a stupid strategy because it might result in their firm's losing the lucrative accounting and/or legal work. For inside directors, it never makes sense to bite the hand that feeds them. Outside directors have no interest other than what is in the best interest of the shareholders. Companies that sell stock to the public

must have a majority of their directors designated as outside directors.

- How many shares to initially authorize and then issue. The number of shares authorized is the maximum number the company can issue. The number of shares issued is the number of shares created when the company is formed. This can be 1 share if you are the only owner. After the initial allocation of shares to the owner(s), new shares can be issued later to raise additional capital for expansion, to reward employees, or to make acquisitions—up to the number of shares authorized. The number of shares authorized can normally be increased by an affirmative vote of the board of directors.

How Do You Find Investors to Buy Your Stock?

Even with the advent of modern capital markets, most companies are started the "old fashioned way." People save up some money and borrow the balance they need from friends, family, and in some cases borrow against charge cards to raise the money to start their company. If they need more money, they either try to get a private placement or take their company public. In a private placement, only certain investors are invited to invest in the company. The three most common forms of private placements are dependent upon the amount of money to be raised:

- **Up to $500K**—Soliciting an equity investment from family and/or friends.
- **From $500K to $2MM**—Attempting to raise the investment capital from an "angel." In most cities, there are groups of wealthy retired executives that make small ($500K) to midsize

($2MM) investments in start-up and small companies. These angel groups meet periodically, and business owners seeking capital pitch their business plans. A good angel will provide guidance and contacts in addition to capital.

- **More than $2MM**—Seeking out money from a venture capital firm and putting together a formal business plan. In addition to providing capital, a good venture capital firm will also provide guidance, help with staffing key positions, and contacts to help with manufacturing, sales, and marketing.

The other alternative is "going public." When you go public, you agree to sell stock to anyone who wishes to buy it—in other words, the general public.

How Do You Take a Company Public?

To sell stock to the public, certain steps are required.

Step 1: Retain an investment banking firm. The choice of firm will depend on the type of company going public, the size of the company going public, the geographic location of the company, and whether the company has a prior relationship with a banking firm. For example:

- Some investment banking firms specialize in certain industries such as banking, high tech, or agricultural processing. For example, Keefe, Bruyette and Woods (KBW) specializes in working with financial services firms such as banks, brokerage firms, and insurance companies. If you were taking a bank public, KBW would be on your short list of banking firms to consider.
- A company that owned 45 car wash facilities in Florida and

Georgia and wanted to raise the capital from retail investors to open another 45 facilities might select a firm like Raymond James that has a strong presence in the southeastern United States.

- A company like Facebook that wanted to sell its stock globally would need to hire an investment banking firm that was also global. This would limit its choices to firms like Morgan Stanley Smith Barney, Merrill Lynch Bank of America, and Goldman Sachs.
- If the company got some venture capital funding from Societe Generale (SOC GEN), then SOC GEN would have the inside track on becoming the investment banker for the IPO.

Step 2: Clean up any legal and accounting issues. The banking firm, working with a law firm and an accounting firm, will clean up any legal and accounting issues including:

- Transferring title of any intellectual or physical property from the founders to the company
- Making sure any trademarks, patents, licenses, endorsement contracts, UCC filings, and such are properly filed in the company's name
- Securing long-term contracts with key personnel
- Settling any nuisance suits and resolving any employee or union issues
- Restating the financials to make the company seem as profitable as possible
- Resolving any federal, state, or local tax issues
- Resolving any disputes with suppliers and customers and signing long-term contracts with the same
- Clearly separating corporate funds from the personal funds of the founder

Step 3: The investment banking firm then prepares the offering prospectus and files it with the US Securities and Exchange Commission (SEC) of the federal government and any states in which it plans to sell stock. This prospectus is a booklet that is designed to inform potential investors about the possible risks and reward of the investment. It includes sections on:

- The company's history
- The biographies of the company's management team
- The financials for the last three years
- The potential risks
- How the company will use the funds received from selling the stock—that is, how much of the sales proceeds go to founders or venture capital firms that are selling their shares versus money that will be used for expansion.

The SEC does not approve any investments per se. The SEC's role in reviewing the prospectus is simply to make sure that the prospectus contains enough information to allow potential investors to make an informed decision.

Step 4: Build a syndicate. While the SEC is reviewing the prospectus, the investment banking firm will complete the process of building a syndicate. A syndicate is the group of firms that will buy the stock from the company and then resell it to the public. The syndicate is divided into three groups:

- **The Lead or Managing Underwriter(s)**—This is the firm that manages the deal and is the primary contract for the SEC, the accountants, and the attorneys.
- **The Underwriting Group**—This group puts up the capital to buy the stock from the company.
- **The Selling Group**—This group of firms sells the stock to potential buyers.

A firm can be in one group or all three. For example, a firm can just be in the selling group, in which case it sells stock underwritten by other firms. Alternatively, the firm can be in underwriting and selling groups and both commit capital and sell the stock to its clients.

The typical compensation for a public offering is $1 a share, as follows:

- The lead underwriter takes $0.10 for every share.
- The underwriters take $0.40 for every share for which they put up the capital.
- The selling group takes $0.50 for every share it sells.

Step 5: Solicitation of interest. The lead underwriter prepares a preliminary prospectus (known as a "red herring") that includes all the information with the exception of the price. The lead underwriter distributes copies of the document and solicits information from the prospective buyers about what price they would be willing to pay to buy the stock. From this, the lead underwriter tries to get an idea what investors will pay and how interested they are in the stock. Will it be a "hot" offering—meaning that millions of investors want to acquire the new shares? Is the interest all among institutional or retail investors? Is the interest concentrated geographically?

Step 6: Pricing meeting. The night before the stock is to be sold, the lead underwriter hosts the "pricing meeting." All the major participants (the selling company, the underwriters, the lawyers, the accountants, and others) are present. One last check is made to ensure all federal and state rules and regulations are followed. The final price of the offering is then set. Naturally, the seller wants the price to be as high as possible; the underwriters would normally want a lower price.

Step 7: Offering becomes effective. The next day, the offering becomes effective and the selling group goes to work selling the stock to investors. In an ideal offering, by the end the first day the stock is all sold and is trading up 5–7% in price. If this is the outcome, everyone is happy. The selling company received a fair price, the syndicate gets rid of the stock and gets paid, and the first public owners who took a risk already have a small buy positive return.

Step 8: Post-sale support. If the stock price soars on the first day, the sellers will think they sold too low. If all the stock doesn't sell, the price was set too high and the initial buyers will quickly dump it. The underwriters may then have to repurchase it in order to support the initial offering price. They may then have to resell the same shares over and over until they are in firm hands.

WHERE WILL YOUR SHARES TRADE AFTER THE INITIAL OFFERING?

After the shares are sold, they will either trade on the floor of a stock exchange or in the over-the-counter (OTC) market. See Chapter 14, "Trading Securities," for greater details.

WHAT TYPES OF ORDERS CAN INVESTORS ENTER?

There are three main types of orders investors can use to buy and sell stock:

- **A market order**—A market order is an order that is to be executed immediately upon receipt at the best available price. If you are buying, you will buy from whichever seller is selling at the lowest price—that is, the "ask price." If you are selling, you sell to whichever buyer is willing to pay the highest price—the "bid price." The advantage of a market order is that it is executed immediately.

- **A limit order**—A limit order is an order that has a minimum price attached. For example, I buy 1,000 shares at a limit of $15. This means I will buy up to 1,000 shares at a price of $15 or better. Obviously, if when I want to buy, there is someone who wants to sell for less than $15, I'd prefer to pay less. If only 400 shares are available at $15 or less, then I only buy the 400 shares. Limit orders can be entered as day orders or as good till canceled (GTC) orders. If the order is a day order, then any portion not filled by the end of the day is canceled. If the order is GTC, then any unfilled portion of the order is rolled over to the next day continuously until it is filled or canceled. (Investors are periodically asked by their brokers to confirm GTC limit orders so they don't forget them.)
    - Limit orders can be entered as all or none (AON); if the entire order can't be filled—don't fill any of it.
    - Limit orders can also be entered as fill or kill (FOK); if the entire order can't be filled immediately—cancel the order.
- **A stop order**—A stop order is an order that becomes a market order if a price barrier is breached. Suppose you buy a stock at $10, and the stock rises to $40. You think the stock will rise but want to prevent a nice gain from becoming a loss. You enter a stop order to sell at $37. If the stock price continues to rise the order is ignored, but if the stock price starts to fall and reaches $37, the order becomes a market order to sell.

How Do Shareholders Profit from Owning Stock?

A company may take a long time to grow to the point where it starts making a profit. A time of 10 years from inception to profitability is not uncommon. Once a company does become profitable, the question becomes what to do with the profits? There are three choices, and all three can benefit the shareholders. The question is: "Which benefits the shareholders the most?"

- The first choice is to reinvest the profits in order to grow the company. Reinvesting the profits can be used to grow the company in several ways:
  - *Horizontally*—Growth occurs by selling the same products in new markets and/or acquiring competitors. (For example, Hewlett-Packard acquired Compaq Computer Corporation so that it could service global clients.)
  - *Vertically*—Growth occurs by acquiring the company's suppliers and/or distributors. (For example, Delta Air Lines Inc. might buy a refinery to hedge its jet fuel costs.)
  - *Organically*—Growth occurs by reinvesting the profits into research and development to create new products. (For example, Apple using its profits from selling computers to create the iPod, the iPod's profits to create the iPhone, the iPhone's profits to create the iPad, etc.)
- A company should only reinvest *if* the company has attractive reinvestment opportunities. To be attractive, the projected returns on the new products or services are at least 150% of the return on equity of the S&P 500 (approximately 11%). Given the high risk of new product development, it should only be attempted if it results in a return substantially higher than what

could be obtained by a passive investment in an index. Unsuccessful reinvestments squander hard-won profits that could benefit the shareholders in other ways. For every company, eventually, the opportunities to successfully reinvest run out.

- Reinvestments can be used to repurchase and retire existing shares. If the company does not have attractive reinvestment opportunities, it should use its profits to go into the open market, buy back its own shares, and retire them. By buying back shares, the company reduces the number of shares that are outstanding—thus, the remaining shares are more valuable. For example, a mature company that makes a low tech product like toilet paper has limited opportunity to expand horizontally or to make new innovations. Suppose further that the company stays the same size year after year (adjusted for inflation) but is profitable. If the company repurchases shares each year, the value of the remaining shares will rise despite the value of the company staying the same (inflation adjusted). Thus, a company doesn't have to grow in order for its share price to continue to rise. Note that a company should only purchase its shares when they are selling at a low price on either an absolute or a relative basis. A company shouldn't overpay to repurchase its own stock.

- Companies can pay dividends. A company can distribute its profits to its owners. If a company chooses to pay dividends, there are four key days, as listed in Figure 1.1.

FIGURE 1.1

Key Dates for Dividend Payments

DATE	DEFINITION
Declaration Date	The day the board of directors declares that it will pay a dividend and specifies the date and amount per share

DATE	DEFINITION
Ex-Date	An investor must acquire the stock before this date in order to receive the dividend
Record Date	The date the company looks at its records at the end of the day to determine who receives the dividend
Payment Date	The date that brokerage accounts are credited with the dividend payment and/or dividend checks are mailed

The dividend "builds up" in the value of the stock between ex-dividend days. On the day the stock goes ex-dividend, the stock price normally declines by the value of the dividend. The decline is the result of the transfer of the dividend from the company's balance sheet to the shareholders' accounts. This results in a predictable see-saw pattern, as shown in Figure 1.2.

FIGURE 1.2

Impact of Dividends on the Stock Price

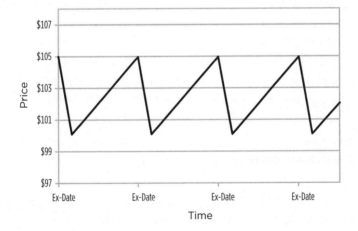

Sometimes a profitable company will do all three: use some of its profits to expand, use some to buy back shares, and use some to pay dividends.

What Does It Mean to Buy Stocks on Margin?

When most investors buy a stock, they pay the entire price. If they buy 100 shares at $40, they pay $4,000. However, they don't have to pay 100%. Under Securities and Exchange Commission Regulation U, investors only have to put up 50% of the price of the stocks they buy. They can borrow the other 50% from their brokers. The investors pay interest on the money they borrow. This adds to the return if the stock offers a total return above the interest rate on the margin loan. Consider the next example, where a stock rises from $40 to $60 in a year:

- **No margin**—An investor buys 100 shares of stock with cash. One year later, the stock price rises to $60. The return is 50% (pre-tax).
- **Buy on margin**—An investor buys 100 shares of stock at $40, pays 50% ($2,000), and borrows the other $2,000 at 5%. One year later, the stock is worth $6,000 minus the $2,000 loan minus the $100 loan interest, or $3,900. The $1,900 return on $2,000 investment is equal to a 95% return (pre-tax). Note that margin interest is usually tax deductible, which would increase the return further.

Of course, margin is a two edged sword. If the stock declines from $40 to $30, the investor will have lost 50% of the account equity—$2,000 to $1,000. If this happens, the broker will issue a margin call and require the investor to bring the equity back up to $2,000. If the investor cannot or will not immediately deposit an additional $1,000 into the account, the broker will sell out the stock and close out the position. Leverage increases both reward and risk.

WHAT DOES IT MEAN TO SELL SHORT?

Investors always want to "buy low" and "sell high." However, the order in which they do those is irrelevant. While most new investors tend to think about first buying low and then selling high, experienced investors often prefer to do the opposite—they sell high and then buy low. They do this by:

- Borrowing the stock from someone who owns it (the investor's broker does all the work involved in borrowing the shares)
- Selling the stock at the current market price with the sale proceeds going into the investor's account
- Waiting for the stock to decline
- Buying the shares back at a lower price and returning the shares to the investor from whom they were borrowed

The difference between the two prices remains in the seller's account. For example, an investor borrows 100 shares of stock and sells it at the current price of $40 per share. The investor then buys the shares back in 90 days at $25 per share, leaving a profit of about $15 per share in the investor's account. A successful short sale! The risk of selling short is that, after the investor sells the stock, the price of the stock rises, and the investor has to buy the shares back at a higher price—resulting in a loss.

Of course, if, after selling the stock at $40, the stock rises to $65, the investor would lose approximately $1,500. Short selling can only be done in a margin account. Investors who want to sell short have to put up 50% of the value of the stock they sell short. In the last example, 50% of the $4,000 is $2,000. If the stock rises by 25%, the investor will receive a margin call and will either put up an additional $1,000 or close out the position by buying back the stock as a $10 per share loss.

Investors who favor short selling believe that it offers two advantages over "going long," namely:

- Stocks tend to rise slowly—but decline quickly. Successfully timing a short sale can result in a very high annualized return.
- Short sellers think it is easier to find stocks that are overvalued than stocks that are undervalued.

Just like for investors who are going long, investors who want to go short have to be able to estimate the true value of a stock so that they can determine if a stock is currently undervalued or overvalued. This brings us to our next chapter, equity valuation.

CHAPTER TWO

Overview of the Valuation Process

The first question any equity investor asks about a stock is: "What is the stock worth?" This is a question that is easier to ask than it is to answer. To value a stock, an investor must be able to:

- Forecast the future economic environment
- Restate the company's income statement
- Create a computer model of the company to study its cash flow
- Utilize one or more of the valuation models
- Adjust valuation for high growth, deep value, technical, quantitative, and liquidity factors

FORECAST THE FUTURE ECONOMIC ENVIRONMENT

A rising tide raises all boats. How well or how poorly a company does depends, in part, on the overall economic environment in which it operates. Car sales soar in economic expansions and plunge in depressions. In an economic expansion, almost every car company will sell more cars at a higher profit margin. In an economic depression, the profits of most companies contract and, in each industry, the weakest competitors often go out of business. Thus, the starting point for predicting how well, or how poorly, a company may do in the future is partially determined by the future economic environment. Thus, part of valuation is predicting future interest rates, FX rates, commodity prices, labor costs, tax rates, and GDP growth rate.

Restate the Company's Income Statement

Before the analysis of a company's income statement can even begin, investors must "restate" the numbers on the company's financial statements. The numbers need to be restated because companies have fairly wide latitude with regards to how they report their financial results. The rules that govern the reporting of results have to be flexible because the same rules have to be used by companies as diverse as mining companies and web designers.

This flexibility can be exploited by company managers to make their companies appear to be either more successful—or less successful. Privately owned companies often exploit the flexibility of the reporting rules to minimize their earnings in order to reduce their taxes. Publicly owned companies often exploit the flexibility of the rules to maximize their earnings in order to boost their share price and multiple, reduce their financing cost, and increase management compensation.

Different companies in the same industry often use very different methodologies for reporting results, and thus their results need to be restated in order to make apple-to-apple comparisons. Doing any analysis on a company's published financial statements is a complete waste of time unless those financial statements have been restated to make common assumptions regarding depreciation schedules, projected returns on pension assets, projected increases in healthcare costs, the value of goodwill, and so forth. For example, two identical companies with $10MM on the bottom line each buy an identical $20MM new piece of equipment.

- The first company assumes a 5-year useful life, $0 residual value, and elects to use a double-declining-balance depreciation schedule. The first year, it would have a $4MM deduction and its profits would drop to $6MM.
- The second company assumes a 10-year life, a $2MM residual value, and uses straight-line depreciation. The first year, it would have an $800K deduction and its profits would only drop to $9.2MM.

Comparing these companies' results without first restating the financials to a common depreciation schedule and residual value assumption would be a complete waste of time. Restating financials is covered in much greater detail later in this chapter.

CREATE A COMPUTER MODEL OF THE COMPANY TO STUDY ITS CASH FLOW

Most businesses can be represented by a computer model that is sometimes called a "business dashboard." These models usually provide a high-level overview of the company (shown in Figure 2.1), and then, by clicking one of the parts, you can drill down to progressively deeper levels of detail. For example, clicking on "raw materials" (RM) might bring up:

- An inventory of raw materials at each production facility, expressed in both units of measure (i.e., tons) and number of days' supply
- The number of days' supply versus the minimum days' supply management wants in inventory
- The expected delivery dates and amounts of future shipments
- An average cost of existing inventory
- Current vendor proposals for additional supply
- Cost/supply forecasts

FIGURE 2.1
100,000-Mile-High View

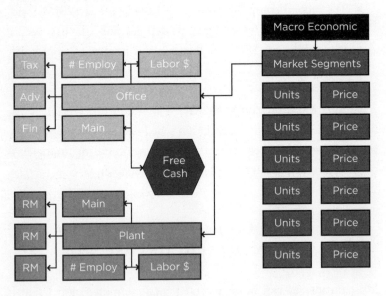

Likewise, clicking one of the company's markets might bring up:

- Forecasted sales of each product in the market
- The forecasted average sales price

- The results to date versus the goal
- Expected market share and major competitors

Usually, these dashboards are programmed to highlight short-ages, sales, and/or revenue disappointments so that management is informed on a timely basis and can address the issues. Analysts create and use these same models to understand how cash, labor, and materials flow through the company. If the analyst has a good relationship with the company, the company may grant the analyst access to its internal dashboard model.

UTILIZE ONE OR MORE OF THE VALUATION MODELS

Once the business is understood, the financials have been restated, and the future economic environment has been forecast, an analyst can estimate the company's future cash flows and value the stock using one or more of the popular valuation discount models. Comparing the price determined by the model to the actual market price allows the analyst to determine if the stock is undervalued, fairly valued, or overvalued as a passive investment. Some of the more common ways to value stocks include:

- Simple ratios P/E P/B P/CF
- Cash flow discount models
  - Cash flow to common shareholders
  - Cash flow to all capital providers
  - Residual income discount variation
- EVA analysis
- Valuation as an option

Different models can result in different passive valuations—with the model that results in the highest value being the most important. Some stocks are worth more than their passive valuation. Stocks can trade at a premium to passive value if investors:

- Are fighting for control of the company
- Believe they can make better use of existing assets
- Expect significant synergies from an acquisition
- Have a strong emotional attachment to the stock
- Believe they can save taxes by converting a public company to a private company
- Believe the company is worth more if it's liquidated, as opposed to remaining an ongoing enterprise

Then the market price can be much higher than its passive value.

Adjust Valuation for High Growth, Deep Value, Technical, Quantitative, and Liquidity Factors

Companies that the analyst expects to experience long periods of substantially above or substantially below average growth require special attention when being valued. Also, over the short term, technical, quantitative, and liquidity factors can have a significant impact on valuation and should not be ignored. All of these are discussed later in this book.

CHAPTER 3

Restating an Income Statement

Let's start by restating an income statement. This is especially challenging because currently there is no Financial Accounting Standards Board (FASB—pronounced "fas-be") mandated format for income statements. The lack of a mandatory format provides companies with an exceptional amount of freedom when it comes to how they format their income statements. While every company's income statement is somewhat different, most resemble the XYZ Inc. income statement shown in Figure 3.1.

FIGURE 3.1

20xx—XYZ Inc. Income Statement (In $MM)

Sales	$123,455
Cost of Goods Sold	($62,123)
Operating Expenses	($17,110)
Depreciation and Amortization	($12,445)
Interest	($8,649)

Taxes	($5,251)
Non-Recurring Items	($2,344)
Earnings	$15,533

SALES

The first line in any income statement is the company's sales figure for the reporting period. This number is the dollar value of goods and/or services the company sold—less a reserve for returns and cancellations. Income should *only* be recognized when both prongs of a two prong test are true:

- The work billed for is complete.
- The work has been paid for—or there is a high expectation it will be paid for in full and on time.

In the case of a retail company, measuring sales is fairly straightforward; a sale occurs when a cash register rings, *less* a reserve for future returns. For large retailers, the future return percentage can usually be estimated fairly accurately from the past return percentages. When restating the financials of large retail companies:

- Compare the various companies' assumptions regarding the percentage of sales that will be returned and make them the same unless there is a good reason to believe the return percentages for the companies should be different
- Determine the percentages of the companies' sales that were only made because of promotions, coupons, or other incentives

However, reporting sales for manufacturing companies is quite a bit more complex because different companies recognize sales at different points in a sales cycle. For example, while one company might choose to recognize its sales when orders are received, another company in the same industry might recognize sales when their orders are shipped, while another might recognize sales when their invoices are mailed, and still another when payment is received. Naturally, when a company chooses to recognize its sales will distort its results relative to its competitors.

When restating a company's income statement, examine:

- When during the sale cycle does a company record that a sale has occurred? Determine whether the time of recognition has changed. Companies that have historically recorded sales when they are paid will change their accounting policies and begin to record sales when the order is received in an effort to appear that their sales were stronger in the reporting period than they were in reality.

- Is the company booking sales while it still has obligations to its customers? For example, a computer company that agrees to provide technical support for two years should not recognize 100% of the sale price of a computer sale until its obligation to provide technical support is completed.

- Is the company recognizing sales that are not final, such as equipment shipped to clients on approval? If the customer can return the equipment, the sale should not be recognized.

- Is the company allowing adequate reserves for returns and cancellations?

- Is the company booking as "sales" revenue from sources that should be designated as "other income," such as tax refunds, refunds from suppliers, interest income, etc.?

In addition to examining a company's accounting policies, analysts should ask a variety of questions like those listed next in order to try to predict the company's future sales. The questions are answered by talking to customers and competitors, examining marketing research, and a certain amount of gut instinct.

- What has been the historic growth rate of unit sales, and how will the growth rate likely change in the future? In other words, what is the size of the market for the company's products, and how will the size of the market change in the future?
- What has been the historic level of price increases per unit sold, and how will the unit pricing likely change in the future? In other words, how competitive is the company's industry?
- Is the company increasing its sales by lowering its credit standards without adequately increasing its reserves for credit losses?
- Is the company robbing its future by offering customers the opportunity to load up on deep discounts just before the expiration of the reporting period?
- Is the company robbing its future by booking sales that actually occurred after the reporting period is over?

Because companies can record sales before an order is paid for, or even shipped, sales should not be confused with cash received.

COST OF GOODS SOLD

The second line on an income statement, at least for manufacturing and retail companies, is the cost of goods sold, or COGS. This entry includes three types of expenses:

- The first type is the cost of either purchasing or manufacturing the goods the company sold during the time period. Included in this category are the costs of raw materials the company used in the manufacturing process, the costs of maintaining the company's manufacturing facilities, and the labor costs associated with producing the goods.
- The second type is inventory losses that occurred during the period. These losses can result from the company's inventory being damaged while in storage, by spoiling, or by theft.
- The third type is the decline in value of the company's unsold inventory due to obsolescence. Inventory must be carried on the company's books at the lesser of either cost or market value. If the value of inventory drops below its cost of production, the loss should be recognized on the income statement. Goods that are "trendy," such as toys, clothes, and electronics, are particularly susceptible to declines in value. Since inventory rarely becomes obsolete overnight, management teams have some discretion with regards to the timing of the "write-down" of the value of their obsolete inventory. Analysts should look closely at a company's inventory in order to ensure that no large write-offs due to obsolescence are imminent.

Another decision that management teams make with regard to their cost of goods sold is deciding which inventory reporting system to adopt. There are four different systems that managers can choose from:

- **Last In, First Out (LIFO)**—Under this accounting system, the last unit of inventory purchased or produced is assumed to be the first one sold. Thus, when a unit is sold, the COGS recorded is the cost of the last, or most recent, unit produced.

- **First In, First Out (FIFO)**—Under this accounting system, the first unit of inventory purchased or produced is assumed to be the first one sold. Thus, when a unit is sold, the COGS recorded is the cost of the first, or oldest, unit produced.
- **Average cost**—Under this accounting system, the COGS is assumed to be the average cost of producing or purchasing the units the company has in inventory.
- **Pools**—Under this accounting system, the inventory is divided into pools based on when the inventory is produced. Management then elects from which pool the inventory came when a unit is sold. (Note that the "pool method" has numerous restrictions on its use and is fairly uncommon.)

During periods when the cost of production is changing rapidly either because of inflation, deflation, or the change in the price of a key raw material, the accounting method selected for reporting COGS can have a major impact on the company's earnings, return on assets, return on equity, net worth, and taxes. Consider the following example.

Suppose a company buys or builds five units of inventory over time for the following prices: $10, $15, $20, $25, and $30. The company then sells one unit for $25. How much did the company make or lose on the transaction? The answer depends on the accounting method selected for defining the COGS:

- Under LIFO, the company lost $5 since it sold a unit that cost $30 for $25.
- Under FIFO, the company made $15 since it sold a unit that cost $10 for $25.
- Under the average method, the company made $5 since it sold a unit that cost $20 for $25.

- Under the pooled method, management can select whether to report $15 profit, $10 profit, $5 profit, no profit, or a $5 loss.

In addition to impacting earnings, the choice of which inventory system a company adopts also impacts:

- **The asset value of the unsold inventory**—When a company sells a unit, the value of its inventory declines by a similar amount. In the last example, under LIFO the COGS is $30, so the value of the remaining inventory declines by $30; however, under FIFO, the value of the remaining industry declines by only $10.
- **The return on assets**—Inventory is an asset. Since the inventory accounting method selected impacts the value of the company's remaining inventory, it also impacts the return the company earns on that inventory.
- **The company's tax bill and cash flow**—Since the inventory accounting method selected impacts the value of the company's reported earnings, it also impacts the company's tax bill—and cash flow.

For all of these reasons, analysts must look at which reporting method is used for COGS and the impact of that decision on the company's results versus its competitors.

OPERATING EXPENSES

The third line on the income statement is the company's operating expenses. This line item incorporates two types of expenses:

- **Overhead or administrative costs**—Overhead includes the cost of maintaining corporate headquarters and administrative buildings, as well as performing administrative functions.
- **Sales expenses**—Sales expenses include advertising expenses, marketing costs, marketing literature, sales commissions, etc.

Some companies elect to report these two types of expenses separately, while others combine these numbers into one overall operating expense number. The composition and trend of operating expenses is a topic of tremendous interest to fundamentalists because today some companies are dramatically reducing their operating costs by effectively using technology. For example, companies that use the web effectively allow their customers to place orders with little or no human intervention—and very little cost. The web has the potential to do for operating costs what the assembly line did for manufacturing costs.

In addition to looking at the operating expenses themselves, analysts also look at any long-term commitments the company has made in order to determine whether the commitments will help or hurt the company's results and for how long. Some of these commitments include:

- Real estate leases
- Equipment leases
- Power contracts
- Intellectual property rights

Long-term leases at below market rates will improve future results—while long-term leases at above-market rates can hurt the company's performance for years.

Depreciation, Amortization, and Depletion

The next line on most income statements is depreciation. Usually, when a company buys a building or a piece of equipment that has a useful life that is longer than a year, the cost of the equipment cannot simply be included in the COGS or the operating expenses (whichever is appropriate). Instead, the cost of the equipment has to be written off over the period in which the decline occurs.

For example, if a company buys a piece of equipment for $1MM that has a useful life of 4 years and a salvage value of $400K, then the $600K projected decline in value must be written off over four years. Just as companies can choose between several alternative inventory accounting systems, they can also choose between several alternative depreciation methodologies. The major alternative methodologies are listed in Figure 3.2.

FIGURE 3.2

Alternative Depreciation Methodologies

Straight-Line	[Initial Value − Salvage Value] / Initial Life
Declining Balance	[Remaining Value × 2] / Initial Life
Sum of Years	[Initial Value − Salvage Value] × Remaining Life [Initial Useful Life × (Initial Useful Life + 1)] / 2
Production Used	[Initial Value − Salvage Value] × Units Produced Total Number Units Equipment Can Produce

The straight-line method results in the lowest write-offs in the early years and higher write-offs in the future. The other methods increase the size of the write-offs in the early years, but at the cost of lower write-offs in the future. Since write-offs also impact both earnings and taxes, the decision of which depreciation method to use is very important. As an example, consider what the annual write-off is on a $1MM piece of equipment with a 5-year useful life and no projected salvage value using the various depreciation methodologies described in Figure 3.2.

Year	Straight Line	Declining Balance	Sum of Years
1	$200,000	$400,000	$333,333
2	$200,000	$240,000	$266,666
3	$200,000	$144,000	$200,000
4	$200,000	$108,000	$133,333
5	$200,000	$108,000	$66,666

In addition to depreciating buildings and equipment, companies also have two other types of depreciation:

- Intangible property and soft assets, such as goodwill, brand names, patents, and the like are also depreciated. The depreciation of intangible property is referred to as amortization. Soft assets must be written off over the shorter of either the property's legal or market life.
- The decline in the value of oil fields, mines, and other natural resources as they are consumed can also be written off. The decline in value that results from the consumption of natural resources is referred to as depletion.

Remember that depreciation, amortization, and depletion are all non-cash expenses. While they reduce a company's earnings, they do not actually consume cash.

INTEREST EXPENSE

The next item is the interest expense. This item includes the interest expense the company incurs during the period and may include any interest income the company earns by investing its cash reserves. Any other income the company receives during the period from refunds or other sources is also sometimes included in this section. Analysts look to see whether the company is paying a low rate or high rate of interest relative to its competitors given its credit quality and whether the structure (fixed or floating) and currency mix is helping or hurting the company's results.

TAXES

This number represents the tax liability the company estimates it incurred over the time period. Analysts will examine this number in order to determine if the company has either understated or overstated its actual tax liability. The actual amount the company paid in taxes can be found on another financial statement, the cash flow statement.

When making projections, consider whether:

- The tax rates increase or decrease
- The company will receive or lose any tax incentives
- The company has any tax loss carry forward it can use

NON-RECURRING ITEMS

Non-recurring items are costs that are both large enough to be significant to the company's results—but which are one-time events.

Some of the types of transactions that fall into this category are the costs associated with shutting down a plant, selling a company division, changing the assumptions in the company's pension plan, and settling lawsuits. Since they are supposed to be one-time events, they should not be incorporated into future projections.

EARNINGS

After subtracting all of the expenses identified above, the bottom line is earnings. It should be obvious by now that a company's earnings and its cash flow are very different. Analysts look not only at the earnings number but also the quality of the company's earnings. The term "quality of earnings" is a general term that encompasses earnings that have the following characteristics:

- The percentage of the earnings that actually represent actual cash. The higher the percentage of earnings that represent cash profits, the higher the quality of the earnings. Actual cash is worth more than "paper profits" since cash can be used to buy back shares, pay dividends, or fund new R&D.
- The likelihood that the earnings can be reproduced the following year. Investors like consistency. Companies with consistent businesses, like Coke and Procter & Gamble, trade at higher multiples than cyclical companies like airlines and car companies.
- The simplicity of the financial statements and the underlying business. The simpler the financial statements, the lower the possibility of serious error, and the higher the quality of the earnings. There is an old Wall Street Axiom: "If the company's financials are hard to decipher, it's because the company is trying to hide something."

As the earnings quality increases, so does the multiple of earnings that investors will pay for the stock. After analysts have projected what they believe a company's earnings will be, the second step in projecting future value is to project what "multiple" investors will pay for those earnings.

Consider the following situation. XYZ Inc. is currently earning $1 per share per year and its stock is currently selling for $15 per share. Since:

STOCK PRICE = MULTIPLE × EARNINGS
$15 = 15 × $1

It is clear that investors are willing to pay 15 times the company's current earnings in order to buy this stock.

If, the following year, the company earned $1.20 and investors were still willing to pay 15 times earnings, the market value of the stock would rise to $18.

$18 = 15 × $1.20

However, if despite the rise in earnings from $1 to $1.20, the multiple that investors were willing to pay for those earnings declines from 15 to 11, the stock's price would decline to $13.20 despite the higher earnings.

$13.20 = 11 × $1.20

Investors often get very frustrated when the earnings of the companies in their portfolios rise, but the market values of the stocks decline. Obviously, the ideal situation for an investor is for the company's earnings to rise and for the multiple to expand, as well. For example, if in this XYZ Inc. example, the earnings rose from $1 to

$1.20 and the multiple expanded from 15 to 20, then the price of the stock would rise to:

$$24 = 20 \times \$1.20$$

This brings us to the question, "What factors, besides the quality of earnings, causes the multiple that investors will pay to buy a stock to expand or contract?" While there are many factors that influence investors' decisions regarding the appropriate multiple, the primary factors include the quality of earnings, the type of market environment, and the rate at which the earnings are increasing, as illustrated in Figure 3.3 and discussed further in the next chapter.

FIGURE 3.3

Earnings Growth Rate

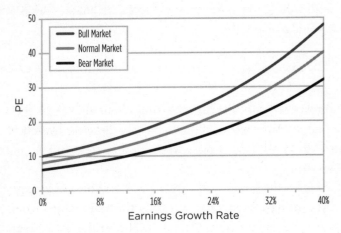

CHAPTER FOUR

Valuation Using Share Price and Earnings per Share

The most basic valuation is the ratio of market price to current earnings per share (P/E ratio). This multiple is easy to calculate and understand:

- The earnings are the value the shareholders receive currently from owning the company's current shares.
- The market price is the present value (PV) of the cash flows the market (the average investor) expects the shareholders to receive from future sales.

The higher the P/E ratio, the more investors are willing to pay for current earnings. For individual stocks, this ratio ranges from 4 to infinity. It has ranged from 10.84 to 29.71 over the last 20 years for the S&P 500.

There are many factors that influence how large a "multiple" of earnings investors are willing to pay for today's earnings. Investors will pay a higher multiple of the current earnings when:

- **The earnings are expected to increase**—The faster the earnings are expected to increase, the more investors will pay for the current earning.
- **The earnings are of high quality**—This was discussed in Chapter 3.
- **The stock is liquid**—The more liquid the stock, the higher the multiple investors will pay.
- **The perceived quality of management is high**—The higher the regard for the management team, the higher the multiple.

The main problem with relying on the P/E ratio is that it is easy for management to boost earnings (and thus depress the P/E ratio) over the short term by:

- Delaying essential maintenance
- Squeezing suppliers to the point they defect
- Accelerating depreciation
- Lowering product quality
- Abusing customer relationships so they look elsewhere
- Delaying the write-off of goodwill
- Stuffing the supply channel
- Canceling training
- Reducing advertising and merchandising
- Shuttering R&D
- Delaying fair pay increases and cutting benefits

If we reverse the P/E ratio, we can calculate a very approximate current return on investment. For example, a company with a price of $25 and $1 in earnings would have a P/E ratio of 25 and a current return on investment $1 / $25 = 4%.

Closely related to the P/E ratio are the following ratios:

- **Price / earnings before extraordinary charges**—Because the extraordinary charges are not supposed to be repeated, most investors look at P/E before extraordinary charges to be their baseline for projecting future growth.
- **Price / earnings, fully diluted**—Fully diluted means that, before calculating the earnings per share, the number of shares is increased by the number of shares that could be added by the exercise of executive options, conversion of convertible securities, and expected stock dividends. This reduces the earnings per share and raises the current P/E ratio, but it eliminates unpleasant dilution surprises in the future.
- **Price / sales**—This ratio is used as a surrogate for measuring value when the earnings are negative. Note that this can be distorted by revenue recognition practices.
- **Price / book value**—This ratio is used when the company has assets or liabilities whose market value is substantially different from the value at which they are carried on the balance sheet.
- **Price / free cash flow**—Analysts prefer this ratio when comparing companies with very different capital structures.
- **(P/E ratio) / earnings growth rate (PE/G)**—This ratio normalizes P/E for differences in growth rate. Stocks with low PE/Gs may offer a better value. Many investors won't pay a P/E multiple that is higher than the earnings growth rate.
- **(P/E ratio) / (growth + yield) (PE/GY)**—The PE/GY ratio adds any dividends to the growth rate. Of course, the multiple depends on the type of environment.

FIGURE 4.1

Buy/Sell Signals Based on P/E to Earnings Growth Ratio

Symbol	Stock Price	EPS	P/E	EPS Growth	P/E/G (Limit on P/E)	Signal
ABC	$600	$20	30	30%	1	Hold
XYZ	$20	$0.50	40	10%	4	Sell
MNO	$100	$10	10	15%	.6667	Buy

CHAPTER FIVE

Discounted Cash Flow Analysis

Let's start with a company that has no debt or preferred equity and is most valuable operating as it is currently. Since the stock is worth the PV of the future reproducible free cash flows it is going to generate for its shareholders, the first step is to build a model to identify the cash flows available to the equity owner. For a time period this will be:

SALES REVENUE

- Less cost of goods
- Less operational costs
- Less depreciation, depletion, and any goodwill write-offs (even though these are non-cash charges, long-term investors will bear the costs)
- Less taxes
- Less debt service
- Less other income
- Less preferred dividends

Cash available to common shareholders / the number of shares issued and outstanding = cash available to shareholder

Example 1

Let's start with a company that generates $2 per year per share and assume the stockholder wants to earn a 10% return.

Number of Cash Flows	Payment	Present Value
1	$2.00	$1.82
2	$2.00	$1.65
3	$2.00	$1.50
4	$2.00	$1.37
55	$2.00	$0.01
60	$2.00	$0.01
61	$2.00	$0.01
62	$2.00	$0.01
63*	$2.00	$0.00

*In year 63 and beyond, the PV of the dividend rounds to less than $0.01. In this case, since the cash flow that is available to the shareholder is the same each year, the answer can simply be found by dividing the $2.00 / $0.10 = 20. This is referred to as "capitalizing the cash flow."

Example 2: Increasing Cash Flows

Now, let's assume the cash flow available to the shareholder is currently $2, but that the cash flow grows at a 3% rate. Assume that you still want to earn a 10% return. The value will then be:

$$\text{Value} = \frac{CF_1}{(1+r)} + \frac{CF_1(1+g)}{(1+r)^2} + \frac{CF_1(1+g)^2}{(1+r)^3} + \cdots + \frac{CF_1(1+g)^\infty}{(1+r)^\infty}$$

Number of Cash Flows	Payment	Present Value
1	$2.00	$1.82
2	$2.06	$1.70
3	$2.12	$1.59
4	$2.19	$1.49
87	$25.41	$0.01
88	$26.17	$0.01
89	$26.96	$0.01
90	$27.77	$0.01
91*	$28.60	$0.00

*Because the cash flow is increasing, its takes 91 years until the PV of the future cash flow rounds to zero.

$$\text{Value of stock} = \frac{\text{Div}}{(r-g)} = \frac{\$2}{.10 - .03} = \$28.57$$

Example Three: Incorporating a Sales Date

Few investors hold a stock for 91 years! Instead, we can incorporate a sales date. On the sale date, the stock is going to be worth the PV of the cash flows available to the shareholder from that day forward.

$$\text{Value of stock} = \frac{CF_1}{(1+r)^1} + \frac{CF_2}{(1+r)^2} + \frac{CF_3}{(1+r)^3} + \cdots + \frac{\text{Sale Price}}{(1+r)^n}$$

$$\text{Value of stock} = \frac{CF_1}{(1+r)^1} + \frac{CF_2}{(1+r)^2} + \cdots + \frac{CF_n / (r-g)}{(1+r)^{n-1}}$$

Note that (n-1) in the last parameter adjusts for last dividend.

Again, assuming a 10% discount rate, the value of the stock is calculated as follows:

$$\text{Value of stock} = \frac{\$2.00}{(1.1)^1} + \frac{\$2.06}{(1.1)^2} + \frac{\$2.12}{(1.1)^3} + \frac{\$2.19}{(1.1)^4} + \frac{\$2.25}{(1.1)^5} + \frac{\$2.32 / (.1 - .03)}{(1.1)^{6-1}}$$

Value of Stock = $28.57 (the same as the infinite series)

Thus, whether a stock is held or sold has no impact on its value.

In these examples, the discount rate was simply set at 10%. While every investor is free to determine what discount rate to use, most professional investors use a discount rate that is determined by three factors:

- The first factor is the risk-free return that investors can earn. The higher the risk-free rate, the higher the return has to be from "risky investments." No one is going to accept 8% from a risky investment if risk-free investments offer 10%. The risk-free rate varies from market to market but is usually equal to the yield on the local sovereign debt. Because stocks are considered long-term investments, the risk-free rate is typically the yield on the 10-year sovereign debt.
- The second factor is the average premium that stocks have returned above the risk-free rate. This varies from country to country and depends on the relative tax treatment of debt versus equity, local cultural issues related to risk taking, as well as the country's regulatory and economic environment. This is referred to as the country risk premium (CRP). The premium is calculated as the premium to a stock with an average level of risk. The average level of risk is usually defined as the average risk of the stocks in a broad market index like the S&P 500, FTSE 1000, or DAX.
- The third factor determining the discount rate is the relative risk of the individual stock. Some stocks have less relative risk (utilities) while others (high tech stocks) have high relative

risk. The relative risk of an individual stock is measured via its beta. Beta measures the risk level of a stock relative to the average risk level of the stocks in the S&P 500. The average risk level of the S&P 500 is arbitrarily assigned a value of 1. A stock that had 20% more risk than the market as a whole would have a beta of 1.2, while a stock that only had 70% of the risk level of the market would have a beta of .7.

- The beta of a stock is determined by calculating the slope of the regression line that relates the change in the stock's price to the change in the value of the index. For example, consider the data in Figure 5.1, which presents both the return of the S&P 500 index and the return of an individual stock over twenty time periods.

FIGURE 5.1

Data for Regression Analysis

Point	Stock	Market	Point	Stock	Market
1	3.05%	2.51%	11	2.22%	1.00%
2	2.12%	1.21%	12	2.75%	3.00%
3	-2.15%	-1.55%	13	-4.55%	-2.76%
4	-.45%	-.12%	14	.55%	.40%
5	1.45%	.99%	15	3.12%	2.00%
6	2.22%	2.65%	16	2.22%	1.00%
7	-2.11%	-1.98%	17	.12%	-35%
8	-1.65%	-1.44%	18	4.12%	3.76%
9	.22%	0%	19	-2.87%	-1.87%
10	-3.66%	-2.78%	20	-.90%	-1.11%

First, just by examining the data, it is clear that the stock is more volatile than the market as a whole. When the market is up, the stock is generally up more. When the market is down, the stock generally declines more. By performing a regression analysis on the data, the relationship between the return of the market and the stock can be determined, as shown in Figure 5.2.

FIGURE 5.2

Regression Analysis to Determine the Beta

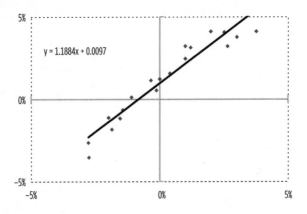

By calculating the regression formula, we can determine that, on average, every time the market rises (or falls) by 1%, this stock will rise (or fall) on average by 1.1884%. Thus, the beta of this stock is 1.1884. In other words, the stock is 18.84% more volatile than the market as a whole. An investor would find this stock to be very attractive when the market is rising, since it will probably rise 18.84% more than the market as a whole. It would be equally unattractive to investors when the market is declining, since the stock will fall 18.84% more than the market as a whole.

Another way of defining beta is that the beta measures the "sensitivity of the price of the stock to market movements." One of the oldest Wall Street Adages is that "a rising tide raises all boats." In other words, when the market goes up, almost all stocks rise—and when the market falls, almost all stocks decline. However, while a rising or falling market causes the price of most stocks to rise or fall, they don't all rise or fall by the same amount. Beta measures how sensitive the market value of a stock is to a rise or fall in the market.

Beta is especially important to clients who want to time the market. Market timers invest in stocks (especially high beta stocks) when they believe the market is going to rise and sell out of stocks (or shift to low beta stocks) when they expect the market to decline.

Expressed another way, the total risk of a stock is sometimes divided into two components: systematic risk and non-systematic risk.

Putting It All Together

For example, in the United States, suppose:

- The yield on the 10-year US Treasury was 4%
- The historic ERP was 6.5%
- The relative risk of the individual stock was 0.85

The appropriate discount rate for cash flows for this stock would be: $[4\% + (6.5\% \times .85)] = 9.525\%$

If, at another time in the United States, you suppose:

- The yield on the 10-year US Treasury was 13.25%
- The historic ERP was 6.5%
- The relative risk of a different individual stock was 1.45

The appropriate discount rate for cash flows for this stock would be: $[13.25\% + (6.5\% \times 1.45)] = 22.675\%$.

If the equity investor earned this return, the investor would be fairly compensated for the risk the investor took by buying the stock. If the return the investor earns is lower, the investor is undercompensated, and if the return is higher, the investor is overcompensated for the risk taken. Every investor wants to buy those stocks that will overcompensate them for the risk they take.

More Complicated Capital Structures

If the company has a more complicated capital structure, then the discount rate used to discount the cash flows available to all capital providers should reflect the cost(s) of the other sources of capital:

- For debt it is: [YTM × (1 − tax rate)] (Interest payments are tax deductible.)
- For preferred stocks it is: [YLD] (annual dividend / market price)

The weighted average cost of capital can then be calculated by taking a weighted average of the costs of the three sources of capital. The capital provided by all capital providers is discounted by the weighted average cost of capital (WACC) in order to determine the enterprise value, as shown in Figure 5.2. The value of the company's debt and preferred can be subtracted to determine the value of the equity. For example, suppose a US company has:

- $200MM of equity (shares outstanding × value per share) − risk
- $150MM of 4% preferred selling at $0.80 on the dollar
- $300MM of 5% 20-year corporate bond priced to offer a 6% return

The cost of capital is:

Equity = 3% + (5% × .8) = 7%
Preferred = $4 / $80 = 5%

Debt = 6% × (1 − .4) = 3.6%

Capital at Current Value

$200MM Equity

$120MM Preferred ($150 × .8)

$265.3 Debt ($300 × .88443)

Total = $585.3

FIGURE 5.2

Weighted Average Cost of Capital

Equity	34.17%	7.0%	2.39%
Preferred	20.50%	5.0%	1.03%
Debt	45.33%	3.6%	1.63%
WACC			5.05%

By adding preferred and debt to the capital structure, the overall cost of capital declines by approximately 2%. This is 2% that can benefit the shareholders. In addition to raising the return on equity, adding debt to the capital structure can:

- Lower the company's tax burden
- Concentrate ownership in the hands of managers and employees
- Encourage the sale of unproductive assets and businesses
- Lower the margin for error

As the level of debt rises, the cost of capital initially declines. But, if too much debt is added, then:

- The credit rating declines, and the cost of debt rises.
- The beta of equity rises, and so the cost of equity rises.

Figure 5.3 illustrates how changing the debt equity ratio changes the WACC.

FIGURE 5.3

Impact of Debt Level on WACC

WACC										
% Equity	100%	90%	80%	70%	60%	50%	40%	30%	20%	10%
% Debt	0%	10%	20%	30%	40%	50%	60%	70%	80%	90%
Cost Debt	N/A	4%	4.1%	4.3%	4.6%	5%	5.65%	6.2%	7%	9%
ERP* Beta	6%	6.05%	6.15%	6.3%	6.5%	6.8%	7.2%	7.8%	8.8%	10%
RFR	4%	4%	4%	4%	4%	4%	4%	4%	4%	4%
TAX	20%	20%	20%	20%	20%	20%	20%	20%	20%	20%
Cost Debt	N/A	3.2%	3.3%	3.5%	3.8%	4.2%	4.7%	5.35%	6.1%	7%
Cost Equity	10%	10.05%	10.15%	10.3%	10.5%	10.8%	11.2%	11.8%	12.8%	14%
WACC	10%	9.37%	8.78%	8.26%	7.82%	7.5%	7.3%	7.29%	7.44%	7.7%

Debt should be decentralized in that each subsidiary, business unit, and division should use the capital structure that's right for them. Each should carry as much debt as reasonable. Mature businesses may be primarily capitalized with debt, while start-ups' capital structure should be 100% equity.

To increase a company's value:

- Increase the company's cash to equity holders without increasing capital
- Maintain the same cash flow with reduced capital
- Lower taxes
- Lower the WACC
- Invest in new projects where returns are higher than the WACC
- Eliminate projects returning less than the WACC

Economic Value Added Analysis

Economic value added (EVA) is another way of looking at the risk versus the reward. EVA is calculated as described in Figure 5.4.

FIGURE 5.4

Calculating EVA

Net Operating Profit	$36,118.00
Cash Taxes (not reported taxes—actual paid taxes)	$2,736.45
NOPAT (Net Operating Profit After Tax)	$33,381.55
Total Invested Capital	$232,022.00
Capital Charge (Invested Capital Times WACC 9.39%)	$21,798.35
Economic Value Added (NOPAT − Capital Change)	$11,583.20
ROIC (NOPAT / Total Invested Capital)	14.39%
EVA Spread (ROIC − WACC)	4.99%

Good management will get a return above the WACC, while bad management will fail. Many investors seek out companies where they expect the EVA to increase. If the EVA is increasing, the company is becoming more competitive. Buying a stock when the company has a negative EVA, and selling it when it has a high positive EVA, usually means a home run for the investor.

Residual Income Valuation

A third variation on the discounted cash flow analysis is the concept of residual income valuation. The residual income (RI) is the income the equity owners receive above the cost of equity.

RI = (Total income EBIT − Interest on Debt − Taxes −
Preferred Dividends) − (Equity × (RFR + (CRP × Beta)))

For a company that had:

EBIT: $1MM
Debt: $5MM at 8%
Tax Rate: 20%
Preferred: $2MM at 5%
Beta: 1.2
Equity: $1MM (100,000 shares at $10)
RFR: 4%
CRP: 8%
RI: $1MM − $400K Interest = $600K Taxable Income
$600K − 20% Taxes ($120K) = $480K After-Tax Income
$480K − Preferred Charge ($2MM at 5%) $100K = $380K
Equity Charge $1MM × (4% + (8% × 1.2)) = $136
$380K − $136K = $244K RI

The RI for the future years should be discounted at the cost of equity and should be added to the value of equity.

Management Compensation

Managers should be paid a percentage of the return (without limits) they generate above the cost of capital plus a spread to compensate shareholders. Never compensate senior management based on outperforming a budget because managers can manipulate their business's budgets and results. Ideally, managers should buy a large number of long-dated "at the money options" with a strike price that escalates at the cost of capital. This means management not only has some skin in the game but also profits only with the shareholders. A flawed compensation arrangement with management can damage share price.

BREAKUP/LIQUIDATION VALUE

Sometimes a company generates so little cash flow from its assets that the present value of the future cash flows available to the shareholders is significantly less than the amount that they could realize from selling the assets and settling all liabilities. This situation happens when:

- A company with a successful past has products that become obsolete. The company may have paid off its headquarters buildings and its plants, but its products are no longer selling due to obsolescence. The company's real estate may be worth more to a third party buyer than the business is as an ongoing enterprise.
- A company has substantial real estate assets that can be developed or used for a more lucrative purpose. A timber company might own land along the shore that may have a better use as a community of hotels, marinas, and homes than as acreage for timber. Since the management of the timber company may have no experience in property development, they might be better off liquidating the timber company by selling the assets to a property development company.

CHAPTER SIX

Relative Value Analysis

In addition to the absolute valuation analysis discussed in Chapter 5, there is completely separate type of analysis which is popular with certain investors. These investors believe that it is impossible to determine a fair absolute value since doing so requires successfully forecasting both macroeconomic factors, such as GDP, interest rates, and FX rates, and microeconomic factors, such as unit sales, price increases, and market shares. They believe that since these inputs can't be accurately predicted, absolute values can't be accurately predicted. Instead, they believe investors should determine the "relative value" of a company as it compares to its competitors in its industry.

For example, instead of trying to accurately value the various airlines, such as United, Delta, Southwest, or JetBlue, analysts who do relative analysis simply try and determine which airline is the best value. This means determining:

- Which has the most lucrative flight routes
- Which has the best management

- Which has the newest, more fuel efficient planes
- Which has the most loyal flyers
- Which has the best employee relations
- Which has the best fuel cost hedging program
- Which has the best plane maintenance program
- Which has the best code-sharing program
- Which has the best hub locations
- Which has the best feeder routes
- Which has the most favorable government regulations
- Which has the best relationship with the plane manufacturers

After determining those items, the analyst factors in the price of the stock. If the best airline is 5% better than the second best airline, but the stock is twice as expensive (trades at twice the P/E ratio), then the second best airline is clearly a better value.

By buying the airline that constitutes the best relative value, analysts believe they own the airline stock that will outperform when market conditions are favorable to airlines—and will underperform the least when market conditions are unfavorable. Following this same logic, buying the best relative auto company, oil company, telecom company, entertainment company, or gold mining company should result in a portfolio that outperforms the market on a relative basis, even if absolute performance is poor or unpredictable. People who invest on a relative basis generally stay fully invested and don't try to time the market.

To compare companies in the same industry relative value, investors use a variety of financial ratios. These ratios are divided into categories and each ratio provides some insight into a company and its relative attractiveness.

EARNING RATIOS

Earnings are the goal of every public company. Obtaining them is the goal of starting and building a business. Comparing the earnings to various numbers helps to understand how successful the company is at generating profits from its sales, assets, equity, and capital:

- **Earnings / sales**—What percentage (if any) of the sales revenue makes it to the bottom line? This ratio can be used to determine if sales prices are optimized. If the company's prices are too low, the profit margin will suffer and earnings will be depressed. If the company's price is too high, unit sales will suffer; again, earnings will be depressed. Setting the optimal prices for goods and services is part science and part art form, and management must constantly adjust prices for market and competitive conditions. Airlines are the leaders in sales price management. Airlines can change the price of a "seat" ten times a day based on demand in the competitive environment. While looking for tickets online, it is not uncommon to see: "last ticket at this price" as an inducement to buy immediately.
- **Earnings / assets**—What percentage of the company's investment in assets is turned into profits each year? If this ratio is low relative to its competitors, then assets that aren't producing an adequate return should be sold. If this ratio is very high on a relative basis, capital should be raised to acquire additional assets.
- **Earnings / equity**—Too much equity lowers the ROE and suggests that equity should be returned to investors. If this ratio is very high, the company may have too much debt and more equity should be raised.
- **Earnings / capital**—If this ratio is relatively low, projects with a return below the WACC should be shuttered and capital

should be reduced. If this ratio is relatively high, the company may be undercapitalized.

- **Gross income / sales ratio**—Also known as the gross margin, this ratio measures a company's power relative to its customers and suppliers. If the company has pricing power with its customers, it will be able to charge a large markup over its costs. When the company has pricing power with its suppliers, it will be able to hold down its costs. Having power relative to both customers and suppliers allows a company to maintain a high profit margin. This is the most important ratio for growth stock buyers because, when this margin collapses, it is only a matter of time until the bottom line margin shrinks.

LIQUIDITY

Liquidity is the lifeblood of any business. Liquidity allows businesses to meet their obligations in a timely manner, exploit business opportunities, recover from mistakes, and respond to challenges from competitors. When calculating a company's liquidity, always subtract any compensating balances. Compensating balances are the non-interest-bearing deposits that a company agrees to make in exchange for a bank providing no-cost services, such as cashing employee checks, maintaining lock boxes for accelerating receivables, and wiring money. Do include any irrevocable lines of credit. Different types of businesses require different amounts of liquidity, so the values for "safe" ratios listed below are just general guidelines— liquidity is best evaluated on a relative basis:

- **Current assets / current liabilities**—This ratio is commonly known as the current ratio; typically, 2:1 is considered a safe value.

- **Current assets / (current liabilities – inventory)**—When analyzing liquidity using this ratio, commonly known as the quick ratio, 1:1 generally is considered a safe value.
- **Cash / monthly expenses**—Once a company has enough cash to pay its bills for 6 months, it should probably put its cash to a more productive use.

FINANCIAL STRENGTH

A company's financial strength indicates how easily it will be able to weather economic adversity and/or exploit opportunities to expand, either horizontally or vertically. The measures of "financial strength" listed below become progressively more comprehensive and inclusive:

- **EBITDA / interest coverage**—Known as the interest coverage ratio, this measure defines how many times the company's free cash can cover the annual interest expense. The safe value depends on the volatility of the EBITDA (Earnings Before Interest, Taxes, Depreciation, and Amortization), the coupon, and term of the debt. The cost of floating rate debt is less certain and increases risk. Short-term debt has to be rolled over, which increases risk. Thus, a company with long-maturity, fixed-rate debt has less risk than its competitors.
- **Debt / capital** and **debt / equity**—The safe value for these ratios depends on the volatility of the company's value. They are used to estimate the company's ability to expand without risking bankruptcy.
- **EBITDA / fixed charges**—The fixed charge ratio expands the definition of debt to include rent, license fees, property taxes, utilities, and other mandatory charges. Sometimes compa-

nies that claim to be "debt free" have massive fixed charges—especially if they rent their headquarters.

- **Free cash flow / total debt**—Low values raise questions. Is the company capable of paying off its debt if it chooses to do so? How many years would it take to pay off the debt if the company elected to do so versus the average life of the debt. If the company does not generate enough cash to pay off its debt, but does generate enough to service it (pay the interest), the company requires an additional level of scrutiny.

- **Is the company generating or consuming cash?** A company that is generating net cash is not dependent upon obtaining new financing to survive and so is less vulnerable to rising real interest rates.

- **Altman Z-Score**—Perhaps the best measure of financial strength is the Altman Z-Score. This is a comprehensive measure of financial strength and is calculated using the following equation:

$$Z = 1.2A + 1.4B + 3.3C + .8D + E$$

Where:
- A = Current Ratio / Total Assets (a measure of liquidity)
- B = Retained Earnings / Total Assets (a measure of financial strength)
- C = EBIT / Total Assets (a measure of coverage ratio)
- D = Equity / Total Liabilities (a measure of financial strength)
- E = Sales / Total Assets (a measure of revenue)

A Z-score above 3 means there is little to worry about. A Z-score below 1.8 suggests a high probability of bankruptcy.

ACTIVITY RATIOS

The activity ratios listed next illustrate how often a company's cash and inventory are "turned over" in a year. Newspapers and their vendors have daily turnover. They produce and sell their product the same day. Cash is not tied up in inventory. Another example of a company with a high activity ratio is a bakery whose goods turn over daily. A parts store for rare cars may turn over its inventory, on average, once every three years. For companies in the same industry, faster turnover is better.

- **Inventory turnover = Cost of goods sold / inventory**—Inventory items can be optimized as a function of turnover and profitability. Items that turn over quickly can be sold at a low profit while items that turn over infrequently require a higher profit margin.
- **Collection period = Accounts receivable / daily sales**—The lower this ratio is, the less capital the firm needs to finance its operations.
- **Fixed asset turnover = Sales / fixed assets (land, building, and equipment)**—If this is substantially below average, the company has office space that is too large or has equipment it is underutilizing.
- **Total asset turnover = Sales / total assets**—If this is substantially below average, the company has assets it is not using effectively.

Investment Ratios

The investment ratios examine the amount the company is investing in equipment, R&D, and marketing. Investments today can result in higher earnings tomorrow. Investment ratios include:

- **Capital expenditures / depreciation**—If capital expenditures are less than depreciation, the company may not be investing enough in new equipment. Note that if the cost of new equipment is declining rapidly (as was the case with color printers), then the company may be adequately reinvesting even if capital expenditures decline.
- **Capital expenditures / cash flow**—Can the company pay for the expenditures out of cash flow—or do they have to secure additional financing or raise additional capital?

Limits on Ratio Analysis

Simply noting that a company's ratio has changed, or that the difference in ratios for two companies has changed, is not enough. It's essential to know the reason why the ratio changed or is different. For example, suppose a company's current ratio (current assets / current liabilities) changes from 2 to 3, as shown in Figure 6.1. The increase could be the result of increased liquidity, which would be good.

FIGURE 6.1

True Increased Liquidity

	Year 1	Year 2
Current Assets	200	225
Current Liability	100	75
Current Ratio	2	3

Or the increase could be the result of selling, but not restocking inventory—a clear manipulation of this ratio, as shown in Figure 6.2.

FIGURE 6.2

Failure of Current Ratio

	Year 1	Year 2
Current Assets	200	150
Current Liability	100	50
Current Ratio	2	3

It is possible to convert many ratios into indices. Indices can convey even more information. Consider the three companies depicted in Figure 6.3. Assuming they all have current liabilities of $50MM, then all three companies have the same current ratio (2:1). However, while they all have the same current ratio, they are not all equally liquid. Company 1 has most of its current assets in the form of cash—and nothing is more liquid than cash—while Company 3 has most of its current assets in raw materials. Those raw materials are a long way from being turned into cash, since they first have to be turned into finished goods.

FIGURE 6.3

Three Companies with Same Current Ratio

	Company 1	Company 2	Company 3
Cash	$70	$35	$10
AR	$10	$35	$20
Inventory:			
Raw Materials	$2	$10	$40
In Progress	$6	$10	$25
Finished Goods	$12	$10	$5

To build an index multiply each amount in Figure 6.3 by the time it takes to convert the item to cash. For example:

- Cash is already in the form of cash so it is multiplied by 0.
- Finished goods take 60 day to become cash (30 days to sell plus 30 days to collect).
- Raw materials take 120 days to become cash.

The days to cash are then totaled and divided by the cash amount. The lower the number, the more liquid the company, as illustrated for Company 1 and Company 3 in Figure 6.4.

FIGURE 6.4

Liquidity Index

	Days	Co. 1	P	Co. 3	P
Cash	0	$70	0	$10	0
AR	30	$10	300	$20	600
Inventory:					
Raw Materials	120	$2	240	$40	4800
In Progress	90	$6	540	$25	2250
Finished Goods	60	$12	720	$5	300
Total		$100	1800	$100	7950
Score			18		79.5

VALUING STOCKS USING
OPTION PRICING MODELS

Still another way to value equity is to value it as an option. To value equity as an option, use a standard equity pricing model: the binomial pricing model introduced by Cox, Ross, and Rubenstein; the Black-Scholes formula; or the Hull-White model are commonly used. For the inputs, use these values:

- The risk-free rate is the 30-year Treasury yield. Use the long-term rate because equity is perpetual.
- The time to expiration is 30 years.
- The market value equals present value of future cash flows available to shareholders *or* the present value of all cash flows available to capital providers—and then subtract the value of the debt and any preferred.
- The volatility equals the historic volatility of the stock.
- The strike price equals 0.

The result is then reduced for any anticipated dilution.

ACQUISITION PRICING

A company may be worth more to another company than it is to passive shareholders. For example, suppose:

- Company A makes doughnuts and delivers them to thousands of locations in New York, New Jersey, and Connecticut. Company B makes various breads and delivers them to the same thousands of locations in New York, New Jersey, and Connecticut. Each company has an 8% pre-tax profit margin. Clearly, by merging, the same delivery trucks could deliver bread and donuts. Product line expansion is one of the principal drivers of mergers and acquisitions. Examples include food distributors and auto parts manufacturers.

- Company C sells plumbing supplies in New York, New Jersey, and Connecticut. Company D sells plumbing supplies in Pennsylvania, Delaware, and Maryland. By merging, they could eliminate one of the company's home office staffs. The combined company only needs one CFO, one CIO, one head of HR, one head of purchasing, and so on. In addition, a merger would allow better inventory management. Territory expansion is another one of the primary drivers for mergers and acquisitions. Examples include banks, airlines, computer manufacturers, and cable companies.

- Company E buys parts from Company F. As time passes, Company E becomes a bigger and bigger customer of Company F. At some point, it may make sense for Company E to buy Company F and vertically integrate the company. In addition to eliminating Company F's profit margin from its costs, Company E can control Company F's inventory management, product development, and shipping priorities. Vertical integration is another driver for mergers and acquisitions.

Regardless of the driver(s) for the acquisition, the combination of expected savings and increased revenue (the synergies) makes the company worth more to a party that can exploit the synergies than it is to a passive investor.

Impact of Events on Pricing

Events are significant changes that act as catalysts on the value of a company. While significant, they usually are one-time events. Here are some typical events:

- Change in CEO or company management
- Change in company size, strategy, or focus
- Change in board composition
- Change in activist interest
- Change in ownership profile
- Change in the company's organizational structure
- Change in capital structure or the cost of capital
- Change in a significant government policy or regulation
- Change in consumer preferences
- Change in a Fed policy

Some investors focus on trying to anticipate events and position themselves accordingly.

CHAPTER SEVEN

Value Stocks

One of the most common debates among investors is whether it is better to invest in growth stocks or value stocks. Look at Figure 7.1, which plots the *relative* performance of growth stocks versus value stocks over the long term. Since it plots relative performance, if over a year, growth stocks outperform, value stocks must, by definition, underperform. The degree to which one segment outperforms equals the amount by which the other underperforms. The average of the relative out-/underperformance of the two segments is always zero—meaning the average always equals the market's return.

FIGURE 7.1

Typical Chart Showing Performance of Value vs. Growth Indices over the Years

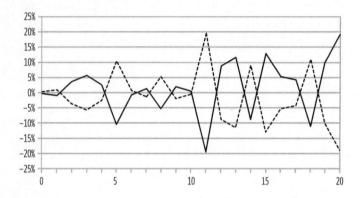

At first glance, Figure 7.1 suggests that, while over the short term either growth or value stocks outperforms, over the long term, it makes no difference whether you invest in growth or value stocks. However, upon closer inspection, Figure 7.1 does not support this conclusion.

The reason it is misleading is because of the way it is calculated. Start with any well diversified universe of stocks (S&P 500, Russell 3000, or similar index) and prepare a spreadsheet:

1. In column 1, list the stocks ranked by either P/E ratio or P/B ratio with the company with the highest ratio ranked as number one—down to the company with the lowest ratio at the bottom.
2. In column 2, put the company's market cap (number of market shares authorized times current value).
3. In column 3, starting at the top and working down, total the cumulative market cap.

4. In column 4, starting at the bottom and working up, total the cumulative market cap.

5. Draw a line where the market cap in column 3 equals the market cap in column 4. (Because the top stocks trade at a higher multiple, there will be fewer stocks in the top group than the bottom group.) Let's assume that your universe has a total of 1,500 stocks and that the market cap of the 300 stocks with the highest P/E ratios equals the market cap of the 1,200 stocks with the lowest P/E ratios (see Figure 7.2).

FIGURE 7.2

Dividing Universe into Equal Growth and Value Market Caps

P/E	Number	Market Cap (MM)	Total Market Cap (MM)
Highest	1	400	400
	2	250	650
	3	300	950
	300	156	564,890
	301	89	564,890
	1498	60	165
	1499	55	105
Lowest	1500	50	50

Allow a year to go by, and let's assume that during the year the average "value stock" has outperformed the average "growth stock" by 2%. Now, let's repeat the steps. When you get to step 4 and draw the line, the line will have to be drawn a little lower to balance the market cap. In other words, a few stocks that were previously value stocks will now fall on the growth side of the line. Now, the 310 stocks with the highest P/E have the same market cap as the 1,190 value stocks.

If over the second year, the value stocks outperform again, then the market cap line will again have to be drawn lower and more value stocks will be considered growth for the next year. Now, the 316 stocks with the highest P/E have the same market cap as the 1,184 value stocks.

As the growth side adds companies, so does the probability that *next year*, its collective market cap will grow at a faster rate than the collective market cap of the value half. This will cause some companies to be sent back to the "value half." Thus, each year as the average market cap of the value stocks rises faster than the average market cap of the growth stocks, the greater the odds become that growth will outperform the next year and vice versa. This annual rebalancing is why it appears that the performance of value and growth stocks fluctuate over the short term, but are equal over the long term. Unfortunately, this is a false impression about how the original 300 growth stocks and 1,200 value stocks would perform if they were simply held for 10 years. In this case, *value would always outperform*.

From the late 1920s to the 1950s, the consensus among investors was that growth was impossible to predict, and therefore, few investors were willing to pay a premium for stocks that exhibited historic growth. Stocks were valued primarily on their normalized current earnings and were analyzed like bonds. Growth was considered to be speculative. If you consider the timeframe, there was no SEC, no centralized databases of financial data, no computers, no convenient way to visit a company's facilities, little market data, and so it is hard to imagine what anyone would have used to try to predict which companies would grow at an above average rate. During this period, few investors wanted the stock that was yielding 2% if the company's more senior debt was yielding 5%. Why accept a lower yield on a more junior security? Since no one paid a premium for growth, growth was "free," and the stocks of companies that exhibited growth outperformed.

That changed in the middle of the century. In the late 1950s, computers facilitated the collection of information about companies and the markets. The job of securities analyst was created, and ever since, value stocks have outperformed growth stocks. This suggests that ever since the job description was created, analysts have collectively been overly optimistic regarding growth stocks and overly pessimistic on value stocks. It seems, the higher the stock's valuation, the greater the overpricing!

In fact, for any reasonably diversified universe of stocks (500+), the 10% of stocks with the highest P/E ratios is almost always the worst performing decile over time. This is one of the market's great ironies. The best performing stocks—those few growth stocks that live up to their hype and potential and turn thousands into millions—are often found in the worst performing decile. (See Figure 7.3.)

Robert A. Haugen, in his book *The New Finance: The Case Against Efficient Markets*, makes the case that value stocks have outperformed since the market started paying for growth in the 1950s.

FIGURE 7.3

The Cumulative Performance of "Value Stocks Minus Growth Stocks" over Time

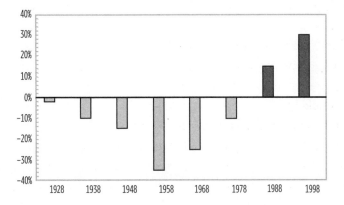

Thousands of studies have been published that all came to same conclusion: Over a 10-plus-year time frame, value stocks almost always outperform growth stocks. In 1966, Drexel and Company published the results of a study of value versus growth stocks from 1948 to 1964. The study concluded that low P/E stocks offered the highest return, and high P/E stocks offered the lowest return.

FIGURE 7.4

Summary of the Drexel Study

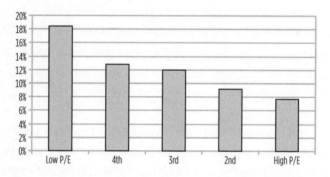

Lakonishok, Shleifer, and Vishny (LSV Asset Management) looked at the period from 1968 to 1990 and came to a similar conclusion.

FIGURE 7.5

Summary of the LSV Study

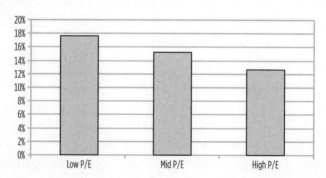

Dreman Value Management LLC looked at the 1,500 largest companies from 1970 to 1996 and came to the same conclusion.

FIGURE 7.6

Summary of the Dreman Value Management Study

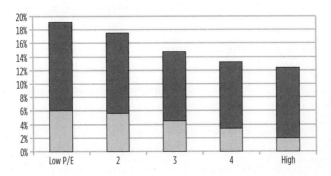

Prior to the 2008 crash, "new paradigm" theories were created every few years. Each hypothesized that this time it would be different and that growth would outperform—and yet again, it didn't.

Theoretically, since it appears that value stocks consistently outperform over the long term, this advantage should be arbitraged away. An extended opportunity to outperform flies directly in the face of the efficient market theory. If value stocks almost always outperform growth stocks over the long term, then investors, being rational, should prefer to buy value stocks instead of growth stocks. Over time, this should lower the return of value stocks until they no longer outperform.

Academics tried to explain the outperformance of value stocks three different ways:

- **Statistical fluke**—The first explanation the academics put forth was that the results were just a statistical fluke. It is possible to get a very long run of "heads" or "tails" even when flipping a fair coin. However, as value stocks outperformed year after year and decade after decade, the chances of this being just a statistical aberration became less than 1 in 248,000.

- **Survivorship bias**—The second explanation was that the studies that suggested value consistently outperformed had to be flawed in some way. For example, many financial studies are flawed by survivorship bias. If you were to do a study involving the S&P 500, started with the S&P 500 that exists today, and then looked backwards, the only companies that would be in the study would be the companies that survived until today. The academics postulated that more value companies went bankrupt over time and that, when their losses were included in the results, that the outperformance of value stocks would disappear. The studies were repeated as forward studies—starting with the S&P as it existed 50 years ago and looking forward. The results were the same. Value outperformed substantially. While there were numerous value companies that went bankrupt, there were also numerous growth companies that went bankrupt—and these bankruptcies were more spectacular (Enron, WorldCom, Parmalat, Healthsouth, and the list goes on).

- **Lack of Risk Adjustment**—After the studies were repeated and any bias was eliminated, the academics agreed that value stocks outperformed, but then suggested that the reason they outperformed had to be that they also had a higher level of risk—and, therefore, offered a similar return to growth stocks on a risk adjusted basis. Unfortunately for the academics, value stocks have less risk than growth stocks when measured on:
  - *A relative basis (Beta)*—Value stocks, on average, have a lower beta.
  - *An absolute basis (Standard deviation, Volatility)*—Value stocks, on average, have a lower volatility.

Having eliminated the academics' objections, *there has to be some reason why value stocks have offered a sustained opportunity to outperform.* In fact, in my opinion as the author of this book, there are at least ten reasons why value stocks outperform growth stocks.

1. Regression to the Mean Happens Faster Than Most Investors Think

If you buy a diversified portfolio of growth stocks, you pay a high multiple for the stocks' current earnings and hope to get years of above average growth to compensate. Over time, the earnings growth rate of the portfolio will slow and revert to the market average growth rate (a reversion to the mean). Growth companies don't deliver above average growth forever.

Likewise, if you buy a diversified portfolio of value stocks, you pay a low multiple for the stock's current earnings, but it takes years for these companies to fix their problems and bring their average rate of earnings growth up toward the market average. The key question is: "How long will it take for reversion to the mean to occur?"

For example, if it takes 15 years for the growth rate of the growth stock portfolio to revert to the mean and, therefore, investors can expect 15 years of above average earnings growth, they should be willing to pay a higher price for those growth stocks than if the reversion occurs over 5 years. Likewise, if it is going to take 10 years for the growth rate of earnings of the value stocks to increase to the market average, those stocks should sell at a lower price than if mean reversion only takes 5 years.

Unfortunately, investors often overestimate how long it will take for reversion of the mean to occur. The product cycle is becoming faster due to the combination of technology and globalization. For example:

- In 1961, IBM introduced revolutionary technology for its day—the IBM Selectric typewriter. Competitors had to buy it, tear it apart, figure out how it worked, do the metallurgy work, create a competitive product, built a plant to produce the new machines, and so on. It took almost 3 years for competitors to introduce a viable competitive product, but by then it was too late; IBM owned the typewriter market for the next 15 years.
- In 2001, Apple introduced revolutionary technology for its day—the iPod. Competitors had the advantage of computer-aided reverse engineering, computer-aided design, global sourcing, and computer manufacturing. As a result, competitors were in the market in 90 days.

As the pace of business increases, the multiple that investors should be willing to pay for future growth decreases.

Likewise, the speed of recovery for value stocks has accelerated. Unions are not as powerful and can't slow down modernization the way they could in the past. In addition, companies today can outsource their manufacturing to Asia, use technology to replace layers of middle management, and do a leveraged buy-out to concentrate ownership. As a result, companies are able to solve their problems much faster—suggesting that investors shouldn't demand as deep a discount today for value as they did in the past.

While it used to take 15 years for the earnings growth rate of a diversified portfolio of growth stocks and value stocks to revert to the mean, today it takes five years or less. However, because investors overestimate this time frame they still tend to overpay for growth stocks and overpenalize value stocks.

2. It Is Very Difficult to Manage a High Growth Company

Another reason value stocks outperform growth stocks is that high growth companies are extremely hard to manage. High growth companies are harder to manage than even "turnaround situations" because it is so hard to keep the various departments "in balance." Often sales get ahead of manufacturing capacity, or manufacturing gets ahead of quality control, or human resources and legal can't keep up.

As a business grows it has to:

- Hire more and more people and often lower its initial high standards
- Work with an ever increasing number of subcontractors. Assuming it started with the ones it deemed best, every time it adds another it is adding one that is less desirable

When the various departments of a firm don't grow "evenly," eventually something falls through the cracks. Quality suffers. As a result, growth stops, the stock price collapses, and the company's competitors not only catch up—but often surpass. (Growth stocks and the factors that impact them are discussed in much greater detail in Chapter 8.)

For example, during the housing boom, the US housing industry exhausted the capacity of US suppliers to produce wallboard. Instead of slowing construction, several US companies decided to buy wallboard produced in China. After installation, they found that the wallboard contained high levels of sulfur, which rotted the wiring and plumbing. All the defective wallboard had to be stripped out and the wiring and plumbing replaced.

3. Value Stocks Have More Positive Surprises

Most of what is known about a company is already reflected in its stock price. Therefore, what moves a stock's price is surprise information that investors weren't expecting—both positive and negative. Investors in growth stocks already have extremely high expectations, so the probability of the company releasing news that exceeds expectations is slight. Any unexpected bad news is severely punished by the markets. With value stocks, however, the expectations of investors are quite low. Bad news is often brushed aside, but surprise good news can have a dramatic positive effect on the stock price. Also, the bar of what constitutes good news for a value company is quite low. For example, a "we made payroll again" press release can be good news if making payroll was uncertain.

4. Growth Stocks Are Overbought Because They Are Overweighted in the S&P 500

The performance of many institutional and retail investors is measured against the S&P 500. As a result, the risk-free portfolio for many of the investors holds the S&P 500—and excludes other securities, regardless of valuation or relative attractiveness. A professional manager who is ahead of the S&P 500 by 2% at mid-year isn't going to buy a bunch of junior gold miners, even if the manager is convinced the gold stocks are undervalued since there are no junior gold miners in the S&P 500. Because the S&P 500 is largely composed of large-cap growth stocks (when compared to the universe of publicly traded stocks), this tends to inflate the price of stocks in the S&P 500—and therefore reduces their future performance.

5. Value Stocks Are More Difficult to Sell

Regardless of whether we're looking at the institutional market or the retail market, most stocks are "sold" not "bought." They are sold by retail and institutional sales people. The easiest stocks to sell are growth stocks. They have the exciting stories, the hot products, are in the news every other day, and their prices are moving rapidly allowing the salesperson to create a sense of "urgency."

A typical growth stock story goes something like this:

> XYZ is marketing a new line of internet routers that are going to render all other routers obsolete. The company's business is growing at 100% per quarter with no end in sight. The stock was $2.50 last month but is $18.75 now. Our analyst thinks it's a $100 stock before year-end. The stock is up $2.20 so far today and could be up $5 by the end of the day. We need to jump in now—is 5,000 shares enough or should we try and grab 10,000 shares while we can?

Value stocks are harder to sell. After all, a typical value stock story goes something like this:

> XYZ makes cement sewer pipe. For 10 years, they increased earnings and dividends at a 15% annual rate. Two years ago, the founder died and his two sons inherited the business. There's been fighting ever since—bringing the growth of the business to a complete halt and destroying profitability. We expect reason to prevail eventually and for the two sons to figure out how to work together or one to buy the other out. The stock's price has been bouncing back and forth between $25 and $28 for two years now. I think we should start to build a position.

The bottom line is securities sales people would rather tell growth stock stories, investors would rather hear growth stock stories, and as a result, growth stocks are oversold and overbought—resulting in their prices being too high and, therefore, their returns too low. Value stocks are too often ignored by securities salespeople—resulting in their prices being too low and returns too high.

6. The Noisemakers Around Stocks Primarily Focus on Growth Stocks

By noisemakers I mean buy-side analysts, sell-side analysts, equity newsletters, and the talking heads on FOX, Bloomberg, CNN, MSNBC, and Cramer, etc. By drawing attention to growth stocks, they tend to cause these stocks to be overbought—again reducing their future return. Value stocks are ignored, allowing their value to drift lower—and their future return to be higher.

7. Value Stocks Pay Higher Dividends

One of the hallmarks of growth stocks is that few pay dividends—and those that do, pay very small dividends. Instead, most growth companies that are currently profitable elect to reinvest 100% of their profits into continuing to grow the business.

Historically, companies that pay dividends offer investors a higher return over the long term. The reason is that companies that pay dividends have to operate with more discipline than those companies that don't:

- First, dividends have to be paid in cash—and there is a big difference between paper earnings and actual cash earnings. Many a company that has reported high earnings couldn't afford to pay even a modest dividend because the earnings are largely the result of aggressive accounting instead of generating real cash profits. Paying dividends is a reality check on the quality of the company's earnings.

- Second, when a company goes through its annual budget cycle, it determines how much money it can afford to invest in business development projects for the next year. In this process, it naturally ranks projects from the ones that offer the "highest return on equity" to the ones that offer the "lowest return on equity." It then goes down the list and funds the projects with progressively lower returns on equity until it runs out of money. Naturally, if the company pays dividends, it runs out of money sooner, so only those projects with the highest projected return on equity get funded.

- Third, paying dividends stops the company from accumulating excessive cash and then making an unwise acquisition.

After a company becomes profitable, it should either pay dividends or repurchase shares. It is the height of arrogance for a company's managers to assume that every project that they can think of is more attractive than the ones that shareholders can find if part of their investment is returned to them—especially since dividends receive more favorable tax treatment than ordinary income.

8. Investing in Value Stocks Requires Patience

While the price of growth stocks tends to be very volatile, the prices of value stocks often trade in a very narrow range for extended periods of time. Therefore, they require patience—something that many investors lack. Too often investors buy value stocks, and then give up and sell them before their price takes off. For this reason, value stocks should be technically analyzed to identify signs of life before purchasing.

9. Value Stocks Have a J-Curve

Investors who invest in value stocks often initially experience a negative return. This is because if an investor buys 30 troubled companies, a few are bound to be errors. There is a wise axiom in value investing: your lemons ripen before your peaches. Of the 30 stocks an investor picks, 1 or 2 will prove to be lemons, and they will go bankrupt pretty quickly. The others will be acquired cheaply, solve their problems, and go on to deliver an above average return over the long term. Fearing this initial decline, many investors (and financial advisors) shun value stocks—again causing their values to be too low and future returns to be above average.

10. Value Stocks Have Less Volatility

Looking at Figure 7.7, which depicts the distribution of a portfolio's returns with a 6% mean and an 8% standard deviation, what return should an investor expect to earn over the long term?

FIGURE 7.7

Return Distribution of Portfolio

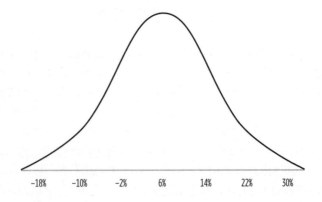

| –18% | –10% | –2% | 6% | 14% | 22% | 30% |

Surprising to some, the answer is not 6%. This is because returns for portfolios have to be calculated using a geometric average.

> Return = $[(1 + r_1) \times (1 + r_2)]^{1/2} - 1$
>
> If volatility is zero, then the return over 2 years is 6%
>
> $[(1 + .06) \times (1 + .06)]^{1/2} - 1 = 6\%$
>
> However, if there is light volatility (±1 SD), the return drops from 6% to 5.7%
>
> $[(1 - .02) \times (1 + .14)]^{1/2} - 1 = 5.7\%$
>
> If there is heavy volatility (±4 SD), the return drops from 6% to 1.78%
>
> $[(1 - .26) \times (1 + .40)]^{1/2} - 1 = 1.78\%$

Volatility is the enemy of return. Value stocks have less volatility and, therefore, offer a higher return over the long term. The volatility can be reduced further by doing covered-call writes and selling out-of-the-money puts on potential acquisitions.

For all ten of the above reasons, the bulk of most client portfolios should be composed of a well-diversified portfolio of value stocks.

Dogs of the Dow

Another value stock strategy is known as the Dogs of the Dow. In a Dogs of the Dow strategy, you start with the 30 stocks that make up the Dow Jones Industrial Average (DJIA) and then buy the 10 that:

- Have had the worst performance the last year, or
- Are currently trading at the lowest P/E ratio, or
- Offer the highest dividend payout.

The idea behind the Dogs of the Dow, as with any long strategy, is to buy low and sell high. When you buy the stocks of companies that have recently "stumbled," you can buy them cheap. While any company can stumble, Dow companies generally recovery very quickly. The reason they recover very quickly is that:

- The boards of directors of companies in the DJIA have little patience and are very demanding of their management teams. If the management team can't quickly turn the company around, the board will hire a new management team.
- Dow companies are some of the largest in the world, and so they have the capital and assets necessary to turn things around. Even the most financially stressed Dow company has resources and assets that would make most small companies salivate.
- In addition to financial resources, they almost all have nationwide name brand recognition, established distribution systems, and other intangible assets that can be exploited.

When the stock reaches market average—sell it and replace it with another Dog of the Dow.

CHAPTER EIGHT

Growth Stocks

Most investors dedicate at least a portion of their portfolios to trying to find that next great growth company, and it is easy to understand why. Truly great growth companies can return 10,000% over two decades to their early investors. That level of return grows a modest $10K investment into $10MM. For many investors, this is lifechanging money. Great US growth stocks include Intel, Kansas City Southern, Oracle, Celgene, Astronix, Walmart, Berkshire Hathaway, Amazon, Biogen Idec, Google, Diodes, Qualcomm, EMC, II-VI, and Middleby.

RULE 1: LIMITED DIVERSIFICATION

Naturally, stocks with very high expected growth rates trade at high P/E, P/B, and P/CF ratios. If you were to sort the 500 stocks in the S&P 500 by P/E, the great growth companies are almost always found in the top P/E decile. Unfortunately, the decile with the highest P/E ratio is almost always the worst performing decile of any index over the long term. The reason for this dichotomy is that, for every successful growth company in the top P/E decile, there are hundreds of companies that fail to meet their early shareholders' lofty expectations. Because the ratio of successes to failures is so low with high-growth stocks, this is one of those rare areas where diversification usually doesn't improve the reward-risk ratio. As you diversify a growth portfolio, it is far more likely that you are going to add losers to your account and further dilute the few winners. Therefore, with growth stocks it makes more sense to put all your eggs in a few baskets—and then watch those baskets very carefully.

Many investors elect to implement a core satellite approach to growth stocks, in which their main portfolio consists of a far less risky, well-diversified assortment of value and core holdings. Young investors might invest 20% of their portfolio in the growth satellites—declining to 5% for investors in retirement who still want to stay ahead of inflation. Once the allocation to growth is determined, the next step is to select the individual stocks.

RULE 2: HOW TO SELECT THE STOCKS TO BUY

It is not easy to identify those individual companies that will be able to deliver desired above average growth for the next decades. The selection process will include all the usual analysis done for any stock, including:

- Quality of management
- Size of the potential market
- Expected capital requirements

But in addition to the usual analysis, the selection of a great growth stock requires an additional in-depth analysis of the company's barriers to entry.

As soon as a new company creates a very exciting new product or service with a very high profit margin coupled with a very high growth rate, it attracts competitors. In today's age, those competitors aren't just US companies but are instead coming from around the globe—from China, from India, from Taiwan, from Germany, etc.

As each new competitor enters the market, it buys market share by lowering the price and, therefore, the profit margin. The existing competitors are forced to respond. By the time the fifth competitor enters the market, the price compression brought on by competition is so great that the industry as a whole only can only earn a market average return on equity and, thus, the stocks of these companies trade at a standard market multiple to earnings.

Investors who bought in early at a price that was 200 to 300 times earnings are disappointed when unit sales soar, but the profit margins and multiples collapse, resulting in a large loss on their stock. They picked a great company with a great product—but the company lacked adequate barriers to entry to keep competitors out. A great product and soaring unit sales is not enough to make a great investment. The great investment must also have a way of preventing competitors from entering its market. Let's look at some of the most effective barriers to entry.

Barrier 1: Huge Capital Requirement

Some businesses simply cost so much money to enter that the price tag alone eliminates 99.9999% of the potential competitors. For example, suppose you woke up tomorrow and decided to create, from scratch, a company to build jumbo jets. Just think about the amount of capital that would take. Let us break the process into three phases.

Phase 1: Design (3 Years)

The first step is to hire 2,000 aeronautical engineers at $200K each (all-in), put them into a nice building with state-of-the-art workstations and supercomputers, and have them design your aircraft. Designers always have to be put on a deadline, otherwise they will design forever. So, you tell them they have 3 years to come up with a design that's a full generation ahead of Boeing's latest or you'll shut the venture down. Oh, and by the way—Boeing's designers aren't exactly slouches when it comes to airplane design, and they won't be standing still. The odds against this first phase being successful are huge (1 in 1,000? 1 in 100,000?) and the cost is going to be approximately $2.4 billion. The rule of thumb for research and development costs is twice the all-in payroll.

Phase 2: Build the Prototype (5 Years)

Assuming that, despite the long odds, Phase 1 is successful and your designers come up with a design that leapfrogs Boeing's latest design, the next step is to build a prototype. Building the first of anything is very expensive because there is no ready sourcing, no tooling, and no economies of scale. You basically have to build a jumbo jet by hand. This means hiring 10,000 highly skilled craftsmen (material specialists, foundry workers, highly skilled welders, lathe operators, electricians, tempered glass cutters, and the like) at $150K each all-in. You may have to go through several iterations before you get it right. The cost for this 5-year phase will be approximately $30 billion—including the designers who are still on the payroll.

Phase 3: Build Production Facility (2 Years)

Once the prototype flies and validates the design, you then need to build a production facility. This means building a manufacturing facility large enough to handle an assembly line for jumbo jets that are each a football field long and a football field wide, buying or building the necessary tooling to construct them, and of course a 16,000-foot runway just so you can deliver them. The flooring of the facility has to be 16-foot-thick reinforced concrete just to deal with the weight of the aircraft. The size of the facility is going to be so large that it will undoubtedly be visible from space. The cost to acquire the land, build the building, and acquire all the necessary tooling is approximately $5 billion up front and $250MM a year thereafter to maintain.

Phase 4: Begin Production

Now, replace most of your craftsman with approximately 100,000 production and support workers (at an all-in average cost of $100K each) to actually build the planes. In other words, you need to spend at least another $10 billion a year—for a total ongoing cost of $15 billion a year. Now, the bad news is that no one is going to buy a plane from you unless you still have billions in the bank because your potential customers need to know you'll be around for the next 30 years to maintain the aircraft and deal with the inevitable glitches.

So unless you inherited $50 billion, this may not be the business for you.

Boeing

When Boeing created the first jumbo jet, it wasn't starting from scratch. The 727 and 737 were already huge global successes. Despite Boeing's pre-existing expertise at plane building, its huge size, and its massive cash flow, creating the 747 almost bankrupted the company. The high risk was offset by an equally high reward because, for 25 years after creating the 747, Boeing had a virtual monopoly on jumbo jets and enjoyed the very high returns that monopolies usually bring. No single company could raise and risk enough capital to compete. No single country could risk the capital required to compete. To finally create a viable competitor for Boeing, nations had to merge their sovereign wealth funds. If entering your business takes so much capital it requires nations to merge their sovereign funds just to compete with you—you have a great barrier to entry. Also, the long lead time necessary to create jumbo jets gives you plenty of time to prepare for your new competitor and it is not likely six new competitors are going to pop up that you didn't see coming.

Railroads

The only US business that, starting from scratch, would cost more than building jumbo jets is building new railroads in the United States. In fact, the cost of building is so high no new significant railroads can be built. The cost of property right of ways, the cost of regulations, and the cost of labor combine to make it impossible to build new railroads. This gives the existing railroads a monopoly. As energy prices rise, trucks will have to raise their rates, air freight companies will have to raise their rates, and railroads will also raise their rates. The difference is that because railroads are so energy efficient (450 tons can be moved 1 mile for 1 gallon of gas) that the railroads' higher revenue will fall to the bottom line instead of being chewed up by higher fuel costs.

Barrier 2: Intellectual Property Rights (IPR)

Another barrier to entry is intellectual property rights. In fact, three entire industries exist only because of the barrier to entry provided by intellectual property rights:

- **The big pharmaceutical industry**—The only reason a company will spend upwards of a billion dollars on researching and developing a new drug that, once it is discovered, anyone else can knock off at $0.02 a copy, is they get a 17 year monopoly on the new drug.

- **The entertainment industry**—The only reason a company will invest $400MM in an animated movie about overgrown blue Smurfs is that the movie comes with copyright protection.
- **The software industry**—The only reason anyone would invest hundreds of millions of dollars creating a new database program is that the program is protected by property rights.

The intellectual property game is one of credits and debits. If the company's credits (new drugs, new movies, and new programs) are adding to the company's free cash flow at a rate faster than debits (drugs, movies, programs coming off patent) are shrinking the company's free cash flow, then the stock price should rise.

Provided a company's development pipeline is full and its R&D efforts remain productive, IPRs can be a great barrier to entry.

Barrier 3: Proprietary Technology (PT)

Proprietary technology can be an exceptional barrier to entry. The ideal example from the first PC revolution was Intel. Intel's early chip (the 8088 microprocessor) was neither the fastest nor the most energy efficient chip available, but it was the chip IBM adopted for its first personal computer. Since IBM adopted it, all the best software developers started writing programs that ran on Intel's 8088 chip. This forced all the other PC manufacturers (Compaq, Radio Shack, Dell, HP) to initially also use Intel's 8088 chip. Given its virtual monopoly, Intel was able to charge a 100-fold markup over production costs (a $4 chip sold for $400).

Naturally a markup this high, in a market growing as rapidly on a global basis as the PC market was in its early years, was going to attract competitors. Advanced Micro Devices (AMD) designed a clone of Intel's 8088 chip that offered identical functionality without violating any of Intel's numerous patents. It then built a state-of-the-art plant to produce these chips. Intel countered by introducing a new chip, "the 80286," and declaring its old chip to be "obsolete"—frustrating AMD. Programmers then wrote for the 80286. As the clone makers caught up, Intel introduced a series of progressively more powerful chips (286, 386, 486, Pentium 1, Pentium 2, Pentium Dual-Core, and currently the Pentium 4 Core).

While the clone makers could play catch up, they could never leapfrog Intel's technology because they would then run the risk of not being fully compatible with Intel's next version. Most software companies on the IBM platform only guarantee that their software will run on Intel's chip. Even today, Intel's tag line is "Intel Inside"—reassuring buyers that all their software will run without any issues.

Likewise, another technology company that set the standard for an entire industry is Cisco routers. Cisco routers are more expensive but, like Intel, they set the standard that ensures reliability and compatibility.

Barrier 4: Reputation for Service

Another barrier for entry is a reputation for service.

The Four Seasons and Ritz-Carlton chains are the winners in the hotel chain space. Once you've stayed there, they are everyone's first choice. They are usually sold out. The only question is how large a premium they can charge over the Hilton, Sheraton, and other chains. In a recession, they only get $30 to $50 over the other chains. In an expansion, the premium can reach $200. Because the hotel is sold out, the restaurants, bars, and meeting rooms also have a high utilization rate—boosting the hotel's profitability even further.

American Express is the charge card with the best service. In fact, service is the only reason to own an American Express Card. Without service, it does less than your MasterCard or VISA and costs a whole lot more. However, anyone who's ever been stuck overseas, or bounced from a flight, or tried to get rid of an errant charge, knows how valuable it is to call AMEX's 800 number and get fast, friendly, efficient help.

Hewlett-Packard's printer division is second to none. Its support line is still open 24/7 and you can usually reach a service tech within a few rings—not hours. The printer drivers work flawlessly and are usually available well in advance of the release of any new version of Windows or Apple operating systems. Many people will only buy Hewlett-Packard printers—regardless of cost—simply because the support is so good.

If you have to send some clients some documents for their signatures, the documents have to be there tomorrow, and a $15,000 commission is riding on getting it there on time, how are you going to send it? The answer of course is FedEx or UPS—both of which have excellent reputations for service—and both of which charge more than the USPS. Why not save a few dollars and mail it overnight at the post office?

The answer of course is very simple: you believe the private services are more reliable and are willing to pay a premium for that reliability. In the case of FedEx, every employee is empowered to do whatever it takes and to spend whatever they have to spend in order to get the package there the next day. The company's mission statement puts it simply: "To get the package there the next day—regardless." The corporate heroes are always the drivers who think outside the box to come up with ways to overcome seemingly impossible challenges and got the packages delivered.

In order for a company to be worth more than its parts, it has to have a goal, a purpose, a rallying cry, and an ideal that it is striving to achieve. This goal can't just be "making money." Making money is always a byproduct of having a great mission—not the mission itself.

Some of the most successful companies had missions that, at first glance, did not sound appealing. For example, Walmart's original mission was to open stores where there were no stores. Now, the reason there were no stores where Walmart opened them was that the people in those regions had very little money. Can you imagine the company's road show? "We build stores where people have no money! How many shares would you like to buy?"

Other companies have missions that sound like clear winners. Netscape's mission was to "open the Internet to the world"—and yet the company failed miserably. A good mission statement is no guarantee of success—but a company that at least knows what it wants to do certainly has a clear advantage over one that doesn't. The advertising campaign tag line "When it absolutely, positively has to get there overnight" reinforces the importance of the mission statement. Companies with a clear mission are easier to manage.

(No offense is meant to the employees of the US Post Office. They are great people who work in a management environment that is so toxic that it penalizes initiative and actively discourages extraordinary performance.)

In the theme park industry, Walt Disney World is the world's premier provider. This is all the more remarkable when you consider that its parks are frequently heavily overcrowded with long lines, the temperature and humidity can both be in the high 90s, and the clientele has an age range from 3 to 100. Yet, the parks are always spotlessly clean, the staff's always friendly, and regardless of the season the plants are always in full bloom. Disney's reputation for service excellence is so strong that the company has a substantial training business where it teaches how to deliver service excellence to other companies.

Barrier 5: Large Installed Base

Companies that have a large installed base have tremendous advantages over their competitors. Let's start by looking at the burger space in the United States.

McDonald's

The largest provider is McDonald's. In New York City, as in many cities, it is hard to walk three blocks without seeing a McDonald's. Naturally, the large numbers of restaurants means McDonald's enjoys economies of scale when purchasing everything from beef patties to signage—but this is the least of the advantages conveyed by its large installed base.

McDonald's first big advantage is logistics. Because its restaurants are so close together, a single delivery truck can resupply a large number of restaurants in a single day. If a truck is resupplying Olive Garden restaurants that are 20 miles apart, the logistics are not nearly as favorable.

McDonald's second big advantage is the return on its advertising. When McDonald's runs an ad in New York (TV, radio, or print) the ad is very expensive. However, almost 100% of the people seeing the ad are within easy distance of a McDonald's restaurant—providing McDonald's with an exceptional advertising value (eyes or ears per dollar spent). If McDonald's runs an ad during the Super Bowl, the ad is very expensive—however almost everyone watching the game in the United States is within easy distance of a McDonald's and that makes the investment in a Super Bowl ad an exceptional value.

On the other hand, if your installed base is not as large, then your advertising can actually backfire and enrich your competitors. For example, on many NFL games, Domino's Pizza runs a mouthwatering commercial of a pizza fresh from the oven with the cheese bubbling, the pepperoni slices sizzling, and a tagline "Order your pizza now so it will arrive hot for halftime." This is a very powerful ad. In my market however, there is no Domino's and so the ad drives orders for Papa John's and other pizza providers.

STARBUCKS COFFEE COMPANY

In New York City, as in other cities I suppose, there are buildings where the northeast corner of the building lobby houses a Starbucks. In the southwest corner of the same building's lobby is another Starbucks. At first, this seems weird. Why have two of the same coffee shop in the same lobby? The answer is that Starbucks wants to have a monopoly on the building. The building has 6,100 coffee drinkers who drink an average of three cups a day at $4 a cup. That's $73,000 a day before you add scones or croissants. It's worth it to pay two rents in order to keep another coffee vendor out of the building.

MICROSOFT

At the height of the first PC revolution, Microsoft achieved such global dominance with its operating system and office software that it was sued by the US Justice Department and by the European Monopolies Commission for being a monopoly. When you're being sued globally for being a monopoly, you know you have a pretty good installed base.

Any time three good programmers get together over drinks the conversation gets around to "We can write a better operating system than Windows." Perhaps they can—but doing so will do them no good. No matter how good their operating system is, no computer user will install it until it runs 100,000+ applications. Unfortunately, no programmers will write applications for it unless it is installed on millions of machines. An unbreakable catch-22. Even Apple, despite having an operating system that was superior to Microsoft's in every measurable way, found out the hard way they were never going to be more than a niche player in PCs because Microsoft set the standard and had such a large installed base. In order for Apple to be successful, Apple had to create new platforms (iPod, iPhone, iPad) where it could set the standard.

Barrier 6: Brand Names

Brand names are an excellent barrier to entry. People often establish strong emotional ties with brands that are hard for competitive products to break. Some cigarette smokers identify so strongly with the image of the Marlboro Man that they won't smoke any other cigarette. To some, the terms "truck" and "Ford" are synonymous. We can all picture the typical Volvo or Prius buyer. A $100 electronic watch keeps better time than a $12K Rolex, but wearing the Rolex makes some people feel successful and announces our success to others—likewise the Coach purse and signature Cartier or Tiffany jewelry. One laundry detergent may be as good as another—but don't try telling that to a Tide or Wisk user.

In releasing the i5, Apple created a brand that was so strong and desirable that it created a mini crime wave of thefts, where thieves would grab the new phones right out the user's hands in midconversation. When your product is so highly lusted after that people are willing to risk prison to possess it, you have a strong brand name. One caution however. When the attachment between a brand name and a consumer is broken because the brand lets the consumer down, the consumer can feel betrayed and turn on the brand. The stronger the attachment between the consumer and brand, the greater the resentment when they separate. It's the most passionate marriages that result in the bitterest divorces. Therefore, brand names have to be managed very carefully.

Barrier 7: Access to Resources

Having access to local resources can provide companies with tremendous advantages. For example, the production of aluminum takes an incredible amount of energy because its melting point is so high. The United States built an entire system of hydroelectric plants to produce the electricity to run the electric furnaces used to make aluminum. Since hydroelectric power was relatively cheap, the United States had a competitive advantage for a while.

In Abu Dhabi, they viewed the natural gas that came out of their oil wells as a nuisance and simply burned it off. There was too little of it to build a profitable pipeline to export. However, there was enough to run an aluminum plant. With free energy, Abu Dhabi quickly became the low-cost provider of aluminum; the US smelters in the Northwest are now shut down.

Today, China has a near monopoly on many of the rare metals that are essential to modern electronics. China caused a stir when it announced it wouldn't export the metals unless it was paid a high export tariff. This was designed to force manufacturers to move their high-tech manufacturing to China. This is in direct violation of the general agreement on tariffs and trades (GATT) and the United States and other nations have filed a complaint. However, as resources continue to become tighter, having local resources will become a larger barrier to entry.

Barrier 8: Government Regulations

One of the most powerful barriers to entry is to harness government regulations to protect your business from competitors. These can take the form of import tariffs. (In the United States, there is a tariff on sugar imports that is designed to protect a few sugar beet farmers who otherwise would be noncompetitive.) Government regulations can also take a more subtle form. In the United States, most crops are genetically engineered to be self-fertilizing, immune to Roundup, have a consistent color and consistent taste, be appealing in appearance, and to require less water. In Europe, many genetically altered crops are banned for the sake of "purity." In reality, they are often just trade barriers in disguise, designed to protect inefficient family farms in Europe from the massive incredibly efficient corporate farms in the United States. The reality is that either for cultural, political, or business reasons, every country has an industry that it seeks to protect. Good luck trying to import rice into Japan or palm oil into India.

Investor Concerns

Every time you hear the term growth stock, you should immediately start to think about the company's barriers to entry. It doesn't matter if the idea comes from your brokerage firm's research department, your favorite newsletter, or your Uncle Floyd. The more barriers there are and the higher the barriers, the better.

If you:

- Read a research report that strongly recommends a growth stock and you like the story but the report doesn't specifically address the barriers to entry—send the analyst an email asking him or her to address them.
- Read the annual report of a company you find very enticing— but if it doesn't address the barriers to entry, send an email to management or the stockholder-relations officer and ask what they are.
- Attend a biotech or 3D-printing conference and a company's presentation impresses you, wait until the break and then approach

the management team and say, "I loved your presentation—but what are your barriers to entry?"

Of course, if the answers you get are poor—"We only hire the brightest people" or "We have a particularly strong work ethic"— then be very careful about overpaying for the stock.

RULE 3: KNOW WHEN TO SELL A GROWTH STOCK

You should monitor the "barriers to entry" like they were dams— look for any signs of wear or weakness—and sell before they collapse. Most investors know that when a growth stock misses its earnings by even one-half of a percent, the stock drops off sharply— often by 20% or more. The first question is, does that make sense? The answer is yes!

To illustrate, let's do a simple valuation problem. Every investment is equal to the PV of the future cash flows it pays the investor. Let's assume the analyst expects earnings to double for eight years. Then, the analyst expects competitors to catch up and the earnings growth to drop to a 5% rate. Thus, the expected earnings are:

$1, $2, $4, $8, $16, $32, $64—up 5% per year thereafter

Given a desired return of 10%, the analyst would value the stock at $772—a whopping 772 times today's earnings.

Let's suppose the company does fine in year 1 and year 2, but in year 3 the company misses the earnings by $0.02. The analyst knows the company did everything possible to get that last $0.02. They used every tool in the business and accounting toolbox, and yet they failed. Since they have already used all the tools in their toolbox, the analyst knows that this miss was by $0.02, and the next one will be even greater and will lower all the future earnings estimates. Suppose lowering the earnings estimates results in a new PV of $462—a decline of over 37%—caused by a $0.02 miss.

How can you avoid being the one holding the stock when its earnings disappoint? There is no foolproof method, but one method that can provide a "heads up" is to track the company's gross profit margin. To calculate the gross margin, subtract the cost of goods from revenue to determine the gross profit. Divide the gross profit by the earnings to determine the gross margin. A high gross margin is only possible when a company has numerous barriers to entry. If one of the barriers weakens, the gross margin will shrink.

With the company that just missed by $0.02, we see the company is running a gross margin of approximately 83% for 6 years and then, in year 7 it drops significantly to 77.75%. There could be many reasons for this, but they are all bad:

- The first is that the COGS went up—but the company couldn't pass its higher costs along.
  - Manufacturing equipment may have reached the limit of its useful life and may be breaking down.
  - A labor contract was renegotiated with sharply higher wages.
  - Raw material costs or subcontractor costs rose substantially.
- Revenues decline.
  - A cool brand becomes "uncool."
  - A patent expires necessitating a price cut.
  - Technology is leapfrogged.
  - A new competitor emerges.
  - The company suffers quality breakdown.
  - Change occurs in trade barriers, subsidies, taxes, or royalty structure.

When the gross margin is squeezed, a good management team will continue to grow earnings for a quarter or two by gutting marketing, training, R&D, merchandising, advertising . . .

A good axiom to follow is: "You can't shrink your way to growth." In other words, it is time to sell!

In addition to barriers to entry, a growth company should have the following:

- A large enough market
- A management team that is up to the task
- A pursuit of growth that adds value
- Sufficient cash flow to support its growth
- Accurate financials
- Growth that is generated organically

Does the Company Have a Large Enough Market?

It may seem obvious, but in order to have high-growth stocks, the company has to have a large enough market to permit it to grow at a high rate for at least several years. This is particularly true with regard to technology. There was a time when almost no one owned a TV. The few companies that made TVs had a huge potential market and the rate of growth that was possible was very high. Eventually, however, the market starts to become saturated and the sales decline. The same cycle was repeated with VCRs, cable TV, CD players, home computers, Cisco routers, DVD players, and flat panel TVs.

The same question has to be asked of every company. From the one that sells drill bits to oil drillers to the specialty retailer looking for good locations, eventually growth has to slow as the market becomes saturated.

In order to support growth of 100% per year over four years, sales have to grow from X to 2X to 4X to 8X to 16X. Is the market large enough that the company, if successful, can sell 16 times as much product, have 16 times as many locations, have 16 times as many customers in 4 years—or will the influx of new competitors cause the market to be saturated before then?

Is the Management Team Up to the Task?

Evaluating a management team is difficult—but essential. Nothing can kill a company faster than bad management. Inept managers are more harmful than competitors, more common than economic downturns, and more dangerous than the government offering to help. There are few management challenges that are greater than managing a high-growth company. In a high-growth company:

- Staff has to be added and assimilated quickly, a tremendous strain on the staffing and training departments.
- Production facilities need to be added and/or expanded almost continuously without a loss of quality, a tremendous strain on engineering, production, and quality control.
- Sales and marketing have to expand continuously, territories have to be realigned, and new layers of sales management have to be inserted, all without disturbing client relationships, client service, or the sales cycle.
- Research and development often have to quickly expand the product line both horizontally and vertically. Of course, the people who used to do the R&D are now often running the company, so new staff is often needed to continue R&D.
- Infrastructure, such as financial controls, accounting, payroll, accounts payable, benefits, legal, security, and so forth have to seamlessly expand.
- Management personnel frequently have to be replaced as their skill sets are outstripped. Often, the people who helped start

the company have to be let go and replaced with people with stronger or more specialized skill sets.

All of these changes need to be managed. Managers in high-growth situations have to deal with dozens of problems simultaneously, while still building that vision that ties the entire company together.

Is the Company Wasting Money Pursuing Growth?

Pursuing growth can either add or subtract value. For example, Microsoft created two very successful products: Windows and Office. Unfortunately, in order to try to accelerate growth, Microsoft also made hundreds of terrible acquisitions. The money wasted on those acquisitions could have been returned to shareholders. Pursuing growth blindly is not in the best interest of shareholders.

Does the Company Have Sufficient Cash Flow to Support Its Growth?

Sometimes a company grows so quickly that it outstrips its ability to finance its growth. A high growth rate always places a strain on cash flow—and often leaves little margin for error. High-growth companies can get into deep trouble when they suffer some unexpected business reversal. In the face of this reversal:

- The company's stock price plunges since what was supporting its price was the high growth rate—which is now interrupted.
- The company's management loses its credibility.
- The plunging stock price dramatically increases the company's debt to equity ratio—violating the company's loan covenants.

- The company's banks call in their loans and place the company in a classic squeeze.
- Vulture capitalists start circling the firm.

It is important with any growth company to do some serious "stress testing." Can the company survive a short-term hit? How large a hit? Does the company have sufficient alternative financial reserves and backup lines of credit?

Doing this type of analysis is more complex than simply determining the "burn rate for companies that are not yet profitable" or projecting the "J-curve" from a new investment. Many a company has reported years of record earnings right up until the time it files for bankruptcy. While rising earnings will cause a stock's price to rise, only cash will pay the bills.

Are the Company's Financials Accurate?

The United States has a reputation of having the most accurate financial reporting in the world—a reputation that has recently been tarnished by the proliferation of pro forma financial statements and the creation of financial statements that are so convoluted and complicated that they are impossible to understand.

Is Growth Generated Organically or by Acquisitions?

Beware of high growth by acquisition. Acquisitions create numerous accounting opportunities to boost earnings that are more to do with bookkeeping than the generation of real value. Growth generated by acquisition is unsustainable over time. Look for companies that are generating their growth internally—that is, organically.

CHAPTER NINE

Alternative Equity Strategies

There are innumerable active strategies which can be implemented in the equity market. In an active strategy, there is always a winner and a loser. Since both sides incur transaction charges, the amount lost always exceeds the amount won. To win, an investor has to have a competitive advantage over the majority of investors pursuing the same strategy. The competitive advantage can be macro- or micro-economic in nature. For example, an investor's competitive advantage might be:

- More accurately predicting FX rate changes
- More successfully timing the market
- More accurately identifying peak performance points in an economic cycle

Predicting How FX Rates Will Change

An investor who can predict how FX rates will change more accurately than the average investor should exploit this competitive advantage by:

- Buying stock indices in currencies that are expected to rise relative to the investor's reference currency
- Shorting stock indices in currencies that are expected to weaken relative to the investor's reference currency
- Buying portfolios of companies denominated in the investor's reference currency when the currency is expected to weaken
- Selling portfolios of companies denominated in the investor's reference currency when the currency is expected to strengthen

Market Timing

If an investor can successfully time the business cycle, the investor would simply buy stocks the peak of the recession (when the economy is at its worst) and sell them at the economic peak (when the economy looks great). Really aggressive investors can short stocks. Prices move in advance of the actual economy, so investors need to buy and sell stocks before the actual economy actually turns. There are several ways to implement a market timing strategy:

- Buy and sell (and perhaps short) a portfolio of actual stocks
- Buy and sell (and perhaps short) an equity index Exchange-Traded Fund
- Buy and sell (and perhaps short) an equity futures contract
- Buy large-cap stocks, then mid-cap stocks, and then small-cap

stocks as the economy strengthens because large-cap stocks tend to move first
- Always own stocks, but increase the margin percentage when the economy is expected to grow

Economic Cycle

Another way for investors to play the economic cycle is to move in and out of different industries at different points during the economic cycle. Different industries experience peak performance at different points during the business cycle.

- When the economy is in full recession buy:
  - Cyclicals—to buy at the lows
  - Transports—to buy at the lows
  - Technology—is acquired by companies to lower costs
- When the recovery is in its early stages buy:
  - Industrials—before their orders increase
  - Basic materials—before demand increases
  - Chemicals—before demand increases
- When the recovery is in its later stages buy:
  - Energy—usage peaks so price and profits rise
  - Financial services—demand for capital/investment increases as businesses expand
  - Pipelines—usage peaks
- When the recession is in its early stages buy:
  - Utilities—defensive during the downturn
  - Entertainment—spending stays strong
  - Consumer staples—purchased regardless of economic cycle

Focusing on Micro-Caps

Large institutional investors are limited to investing in the equities of the largest global companies. These are the only stocks that have the liquidity that large investors require. They need to be able to buy shares in 100,000+ share blocks and only the largest companies' stocks offer that kind of liquidity. Retail investors have the luxury of being able to invest in companies of all sizes. However, since they don't have to compete with the institutional investors in the world of micro-caps, they are not at a disadvantage. In addition, while there are only a few thousand large companies globally, there are over 50,000 publicly traded micro-cap companies from which investors can build a portfolio.

Pure Alpha Play

In a pure alpha play, an investor holds a portfolio of both long and short positions that collectively have a beta of zero. By having a beta of zero, the investor is not exposed to general market moves. Instead, the investor is long stocks where the investor expects a positive alpha and is short stocks where the investor expects a negative alpha. Thus, regardless of whether the market moves up or moves down the investor expects to outperform. In a rising market, the stocks with a positive alpha should outperform. In a declining market, the short positions with a negative alpha should outperform. Because the outperformance is usually limited, investors who chase alpha usually leverage up their positions.

S&P 100 Worst

This strategy requires holding an S&P 500 exchange-traded fund and shorting the 100 stocks in the index the investor expects to be the worst performers. Investors who implement this strategy believe it is easier to select companies that will underperform than it is to find companies that will outperform.

High Dividend Approach

This strategy requires selecting a portfolio of stocks that pay very high-dividend yields. These companies are generally very mature. The key to the success of this approach is to see what percent of the free cash flow—CapX (mandatory capital expenditures)—are being paid out in dividends. Ideally, it is less than 70% so that the dividends do not have to be reduced if business should drop off slightly. Note companies that are paying out such large dividends are usually only growing at the rate of inflation, so the dividend income often represents the total real return.

Rising Dividend Approach

This strategy requires selecting a portfolio of stocks that currently pay only moderate dividends, but where the dividends are expected to grow rapidly. These companies are usually generating free cash and are reaching the end of their rapid growth phase. As their expenses decline as a percent of sales, these companies can dramatically increase their dividends over a 5- to 10-year period. Historically, this strategy has returned the highest return of any strategy.

Covered Call Writing

This strategy involves buying stocks and selling out-of-the-money call options against the positions. (Calls are discussed in detail in my book *The Investor's Guidebook to Derivatives: Demystifying Derivatives and Their Applications*.) For example, if a stock was selling at

$100, paid a 5% dividend rate, and the 3-month $105 call was selling at $7.50, the annualized return to the investor in 3 months would be as described in Figure 9.1.

FIGURE 9.1

Return from Option Writing

Stock Price in 3-Months	Sell Price	Dividend and Premium	Total Value	Initial Investment	Quarter Gain	Quarter Return	Annual Return
$110	$105	$1.25 + $7.50	$113.75	$92.50	$21.25	22.97%	91.89%
$105	$105	$1.25 + $7.50	$113.75	$92.50	$21.25	22.97%	91.89%
$100	$100	$1.25 + $7.50	$108.75	$92.50	$16.25	17.57%	70.27%
$95	$95	$1.25 + $7.50	$103.75	$92.50	$11.25	12.16%	48.65%
$90	$90	$1.25 + $7.50	$98.75	$92.50	$6.25	6.76%	27.03%
$85	$85	$1.25 + $7.50	$93.75	$92.50	$1.25	1.35%	5.41%
$80	$80	$1.25 + $7.50	$88.75	$92.50	-$3.75	-4.05%	-16.22%

CHAPTER TEN

Technical Analysis

Another form of analysis is technical. Proponents of technical analysis believe that by studying the "pattern" of how a stock's price has changed in the past, it is possible to predict how the price will change in the future. Proponents of technical analysis fall into one of two schools: those who believe that technical analysis works because it is valid in and of itself, and those who believe technical analysis works because it creates self-fulfilling prophecies.

Those proponents of technical analysis who believe technical analysis is valid in its own right believe that by studying the pattern of stock prices it is possible to learn, indirectly, what everyone who does fundamental analysis knows about the stock—including non-public information. They believe that everything that everyone who does fundamental analysis knows is reflected in the prices at which they were and are willing to buy or to sell the stock. They also believe that when a stock's price changes, it does so for a reason, even if that reason is not yet apparent—even to the analysts. Further, true believers in technical analysis believe that, by studying the price patterns of stocks, it is possible to gain valuable insight into the current mass psychology of investors—something that fundamental analysis cannot reveal.

Many investors who do not necessary believe in the inherent validity of technical analysis still find it to be useful. They believe it is useful because so many *other* people believe in it and that the collective belief of the "true believers" results in a self-fulfilling prophecy. Their reasoning is as follows:

"If enough people believe that a certain price pattern indicates that a stock will rise, then when a stock's prices exhibit that pattern, the true believers in technical analysis will rush to buy the stock. As a result, the stock's price will rise." If the stock's price is going to rise as a result of buying pressure from the true believers, "Why not go along for the ride?"

Most experts agree that the accuracy of technical analysis increases as volume increases and as the market becomes more efficient. Since large-cap stocks have the highest trading volume and are the most efficient stocks, technical analysis is probably more valid for large-cap stocks than for growth stocks. Investors who do not believe that the market is largely efficient should usually also reject technical analysis.

The easiest way to start an argument among investors is to start a discussion of whether or not technical analysis is valid. There are almost as many opinions as to the validity of technical analysis as there are investors.

Some investors believe so completely in technical analysis that they make their investment decisions solely on a technical basis. They make their buy and sell decisions after examining charts where the name of the company is hidden. Only after they have decided to buy or sell do they look at the name of the company. They believe that knowing the name of the company before they look at the chart would prejudice what they see.

Other investors are absolutely convinced that technical analysis is complete bunk and that psychic hotlines are better sources of information than technical analysis.

Most investors fall somewhere in between. They neither rely exclusively on technical analysis nor do they dismiss it. They use technical analysis to confirm the conclusions they come to via their fundamental research and to help them time their purchases and sales.

While there are numerous technical theories, the most commonly employed technical methodology is the study of bar charts. A bar chart is so named because the trading range of a stock over a given time frame (usually a single trading day) is represented by a simple graphic referred to as a "bar." Each bar can present all of the information depicted in Figure 10.1.

- The price at which the stock opened during the day (the bar that sticks out to the left)
- The low price at which it traded during the day (the bottom of the vertical bar)
- The high price at which it traded during the day (the top of the vertical bar)
- The closing price at which it traded during the day (the bar that sticks out to the right)
- The daily trading range (the length of the vertical line)

FIGURE 10.1

Bar for a Specified Time Period

The bars (shown in Figure 10.2) are plotted on a chart that plots time (on the X-axis) against the price (on the Y-axis). The scale for the price axis is logarithmic, so the change in price is presented on a percentage basis.

FIGURE 10.2

Bar Chart with Volume on Left Y Axis (Linear) and Price on Right Y Axis (Logarithmic)

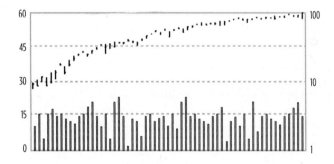

Consider the following example:

Suppose Stock A is currently selling for $5, and Stock B is currently selling for $50. Subsequently, the price of both stocks rises by $5. If the scale on which this change was graphed was arithmetic, then both changes would appear to be of equal size—despite the fact that this would distort the real impact of the price change. If the price of Stock A rises from $5 to $10, its price has increased by 100%. If the price of Stock B rises from $50 to $55, its price has increased by only 10%. On a logarithmic scale, the $5 increase in Stock A will be represented graphically as ten times as large as the $5 increase in Stock B—eliminating the distortion.

Because so many technical theories are dependent upon both changes in price and changes in trading volume, the daily trading volume is typically represented along the bottom of the same chart.

Putting it all together, a complete bar chart for a very volatile stock that generated the data shown in Figure 10.3 is illustrated in Figure 10.4.

FIGURE 10.3

Data for Daily Trading Volume Chart

	Day 1	Day 2	Day 3	Day 4
Volume	20	30	10	25
High	55	70	90	55
Low	20	40	55	85
Close	30	55	80	75

FIGURE 10.4

Chart from Daily Trading Volume Data

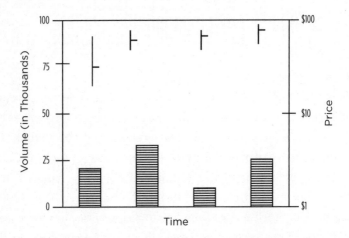

The resulting graph is then examined for characteristic patterns which are believed to be indicative of future price movements. Many of the patterns require accompanying changes in trading volume in order to be validated. Therefore, a bar chart normally incorporates trading volume as well as price information.

It is important to note that investors should only rely on patterns that are both clearly identifiable and complete. Most experts agree that technical analysis will generate too many false signals unless it is approached with a rigid discipline.

Chart patterns can be divided into two main categories, patterns that indicate that the current trend will continue and patterns that indicate that the current trend will reverse itself. Let's start by examining just a few of the patterns that indicate reversals. Any discussion of reversal patterns must start with a discussion of head and shoulder patterns—which come in both "tops" and "bottoms." A head and shoulders "top" is identified by a rise, followed by a decline, followed by a higher rise, followed by a decline, followed by a smaller rise, followed by a decline, as shown in Figure 10.5.

FIGURE 10.5

Head and Shoulders Top

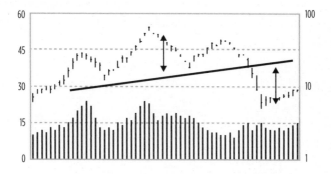

A line drawn along the bottom of the peaks is referred to as the neckline. When the neckline is significantly penetrated, a reversal is indicated. In order for the reversal to be confirmed, the pattern should have the following characteristics:

- It should form over a relatively short period of time (a few weeks).

- The volume should rise sharply during the formation of the left shoulder and the head—but not the right shoulder.

Note also that:

- If the neckline is broken, but then is subsequently rebroken on the upside, that the reversal signal is false. The price of the stock should rise substantially when a head and shoulder top fails.
- If the neckline has a negative slope, then breaking the neckline is particularly negative for the stock.
- If, and only if, the neckline is upwards-sloping, then the distance from the neckline to the head is the target for the downside price move.

Head and shoulder bottoms are the reverse of the head and shoulder tops. The key differences between head and shoulder bottoms and head and shoulder tops is that bottoms take longer periods of time to form and have high volume at the head and the *right* shoulder.

Diamond Reversal

Another common reversal pattern is the diamond reversal pattern. In this pattern (shown in Figure 10.6), the daily trading range first widens and then narrows while volume declines.

FIGURE 10.6

Diamond Reversal Pattern

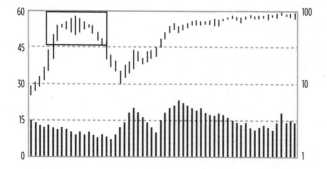

WEDGE FORMATION

Another fairly common reversal pattern, the wedge, is depicted in Figure 10.7. Wedges can be both bullish and bearish. In a bearish wedge, both the support line and the resistance line have a positive slope, but the support line has a steeper slope than the resistance line. The explanation of why a bearish wedge is perceived as being bearish, even though the price is rising, is as follows. Each time the price advances, it advances by a smaller amount, leading to the conclusion that the uptrend will soon run out of steam completely. The confirming signal for a wedge formation is that volume declines as the wedge pattern develops.

FIGURE 10.7

Wedge Formation Pattern

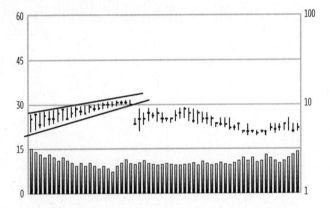

RIGHT TRIANGLE

In a right triangle (Figure 10.8), either the support line or the resistance line has zero slope, while the other line has a converging slope. The price tends to break through the line with a zero slope as the two lines converge.

A bullish right triangle is created when a large block of stock is sold over time at a set price. For example, a owner of a large block might want to sell at $50. Every time the stock reaches $50, the seller sells as much as possible before the price retreats. If the stock continues to bounce back despite the selling, it demonstrates significant strength. Once the large block is completely liquidated, the stock can again advance.

FIGURE 10.8
Bullish Right Triangle

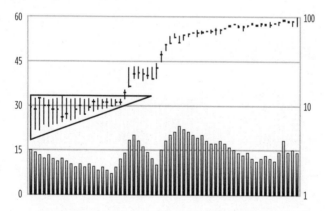

A bearish right triangle is created when a large block is being acquired at a set price. The acquisition places temporary support under the price of the stock. The support disappears when the block is acquired. If the acquisition of the block was not enough to stop the decline, as soon as the support is removed, the stock will continue to decline.

FLAGS AND PENNANTS

During market advances and declines, the market often pauses to catch its breath. One pattern, which often appears halfway through a market advance or decline, is the flag pattern. The flag pattern represents a period of consolidation between a tight support and resistance line. If the support and resistance lines converge, as shown in Figure 10.9, the pattern is known as a pennant.

FIGURE 10.9

Flag Pattern

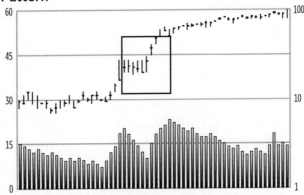

Stock prices often trade within fairly narrow ranges for extended periods of time. The reason the trading range is often narrow is that the majority of investors largely agree on what the fair price of the stock is—plus or minus a small margin. These trading ranges can:

- Be flat, if the majority of investors expect the company's performance to be largely unchanged

- Rise over time, if the majority of investors agree upon the rate at which the company's earnings will grow
- Decline, if the majority of investors agree upon the rate at which the company's earnings will decline

As significant new information becomes known, the trading range changes as the majority of investors change their opinion regarding the company's prospects.

The trading range is bounded by support and resistance lines. Support occurs at the price where the market perceives the stock to offer an exceptional value. Resistance occurs when even the stock's most ardent fans are convinced the stock is fully priced. The significance of the support and resistance lines increases as:

- The speed at which the price moves between the support and resistance lines increases.
- The number of times the stock has bounced off of both the support and resistance lines increases.
- The trading volume increases.

Some additional notes on support and resistance lines:

- A support line can be broken on low volume, but it takes high volume to overcome a resistance line.
- When a resistance line is broken, it often becomes a support line (and a broken support line often becomes a resistance line). There is some logic to this. The resistance line is at the upper limit of the earlier range that investors thought represented fair value. If the value of the stock declines to this range again, investors who "missed it" last time don't want to miss it again and so they buy it at the top of the previous trading range.

CHAPTER ELEVEN

Preferred Stock

In addition to common stock, there is another form of stock called "preferred stock." Preferred stock is a debt-equity hybrid. On the company's books, money raised from selling preferred is counted as equity. However, most preferred stocks pay a fixed dividend regardless of how well or how poorly the company is doing. If a company issues a $100 20-year 6% preferred, it will pay $6 a year for each share for the next 20 years.

The main difference between preferred stock and debt is that the company's preferred is always subordinate to the company's debt. If the company is unable to make the dividend payment, the shareholders cannot throw the company into bankruptcy. While bankruptcy is not a possibility, the issuer usually has other incentives to make the dividend payments on its preferred. These incentives are specified in the offering prospectus and typically include a prohibition against making dividend payments to its common stockholders or bonus payments to the company's managers unless it is current on its payments to its preferred holders.

Companies issue equity in order to strengthen their balance

sheets—that is, improve their debt-to-equity ratios. They may need to strengthen their balance sheets in order to:

- Not violate the covenants in their loan agreements.
- Meet legally mandated debt-to-equity ratios if they are in regulated industries such as banking or insurance.

Preferred stock allows a company to maintain the debt-to-equity ratio they require without issuing additional common shares which dilutes the common holders. Consider the impact of incorporating preferred stock into the capital structure on the income statement for the company described in Figure 11.1.

FIGURE 11.1

Impact of Adding Preferred on Common Stock Earnings

Without Preferred	
Sales	$1,400,000
COGS	$400,000
Operating Costs	$300,000
EBITDA	$300,000
Debt Interest $2MM at 10%	$200,000
20,000 Shares Common @ $100	$200,000 / $10 a share in earnings
With Preferred	
Sales	$1,400,000
COGS	$400,000
Operating Costs	$300,000
EBITDA	$300,000
Debt Interest $2MM at 10%	$200,000

With Preferred	
Preferred 10,000 Shares 8% @ $100	$80,000
10,000 Shares Common @ $100	$120,000 / $12 a share in earnings

By using preferred stock, the company was able to boost the return on common by 20% (from $10 to $12) and yet still maintain a 1:1 ratio between debt ($2MM) and equity ($2MM). The preferred stock can offer a lower return (7%) than the debt (10%) despite being subordinate because dividends are taxed at a lower rate than interest income:

- Debt—10% at a 40% combined tax rate = 6% after tax
- Preferred—8% at a 20% combined tax rate = 6.4% after tax

There are several variations of preferred stock in addition to the "straight preferred" described above, such as:

- **Preference preferred**—If a company issues more than one issue of preferred, they are usually considered to be *pari passu*, meaning of equal rank. If there is only enough money to pay half the dividends, then all the issues of preferred receive half their dividends. The only exception is preference stock. If one of the company's preferred issues is designated as preference stock, its dividends get paid before the other preferred issues.
- **The cumulative option**—If a preferred stock is cumulative, then, in the event the company is unable to meet its preferred dividend payments, the dividends accrue—in perpetuity—against the preferred. Before common shareholders can again receive dividends and managers can again receive bonuses, all

of the past-due dividends must be paid to the preferred stock-holders. However, if the stock is not cumulative, then any dividend payments that are missed are simply forgotten.

If an investor buys a cumulative preferred stock that has not paid dividends in 5 years, and then later the company again pays dividends, the preferred stock owner will receive all 5 years' worth of back dividends. Many investors try to find cumulative preferred issues where the dividends are currently in arrears, but may shortly be made current.

- **The participating option**—If a preferred stock is participating, then in the event the company has an especially good year, the preferred shareholders also participate in the company's good fortune—usually by receiving an extra dividend payment. What defines an "especially good year" is defined in the prospectus of each issue. Usually, it is defined either as the company having "earnings in excess of X dollars" or a "profit margin above a certain %."

- **The voting rights option**—Usually preferred shareholders do not to get the right to vote for members of the board of directors. The exception is when the preferred stock has a voting rights option. This option grants the owners of the preferred shares voting rights—if, and only if, the issuer is behind on its dividend payments. The preferred holder get these voting rights in order to protect their interests—interests which need protection if the dividends aren't being paid. Sometimes, the preferred owners are granted enough votes to effectively seize control the company—again, only if a dividend payment is missed. The details of any voting right options are found in the offering prospectus.

- **The convertible option**—Many preferred issues offer investors the right to convert their preferred stocks into a fixed number of shares of the company's common stock. This gives investors the opportunity to participate to some degree in the appreciation of the company's common shares. The trade-off is that convertible preferreds offer a lower yield. The difference in yield is what pays for the option.

- **The exchangeable option**—Some preferreds can be exchanged for more senior debt under certain circumstances. Sometimes, they can be exchanged when a company's tax loss carry forwards are exhausted. For companies, interest is tax deductible, dividends are not. However, if a company is carrying tax losses forward, there's nothing to deduct against until the carry forwards are used up. Thus, the company might want to pay 5% dividends until its loss carry forward is exhausted, and then start paying 6% tax deductible interest—that actually costs only 4%.

- **Floating rate preferred**—A floating rate preferred has a dividend rate that floats in sync with a short-term interest rate index, such as T-bills or LIBOR. Because the dividend rate floats, the principal value is less volatile.

- **Cumulative preferred**—A cumulative preferred is a preferred where any missed dividends must be paid before the company can pay any common dividends or buy back any shares. If the preferred is not cumulative and the company is unable to make any scheduled dividend payments, they are simply forgotten.

- **Callable preferred**—If a preferred is callable, the issuer can shorten the life of the preferred. The issuer will shorten the life if interest rates decline and the company can issue new preferred stock at a lower rate.

- **Putable preferred**—If a preferred is putable, the investor can shorten the life of the preferred. The investor will shorten the life of a preferred if rates rise and the investor can buy a new preferred that pays a higher dividend rate.

- **Convertible preferred**—Convertible securities are discussed in detail in Chapter 12.

Why Do Investors Buy Preferred?

There are several reasons why investors purchase preferred stocks. Some investors buy preferred stocks:

- **As interest rate plays**—As with any fixed rate instrument, the prices rise as interest rates fall—and fall as interest rates rise. Preferred stocks are sometimes used to speculate on interest rates because of their relatively long durations. The modified duration of a preferred stock is approximately equal to:

Modified Duration @ (1 + Yield) / Yield

For a preferred stock offering a 7% yield, the modified duration would be approximately equal to:

Modified Duration @ (1 + .07) / .07 @ 15.29%

Thus, if interest rates rise or fall by 1%, the price of the preferred will change by 15.29%. This assumes that the preferred is perpetual and, therefore, not subject to being called by the issuer.

- **To generate steady income**—Many investors, such as retirees, have "obtaining a high steady income" as their primary investment goal. Preferred stocks are attractive to these investors because they offer a higher after-tax yield than debt instruments. The trade-off is they also offer higher credit risk because they are junior to the debt.
- **To generate tax-advantaged income**—Preferred stocks, like

common stocks, are subject to the 70% dividend exclusion rule. When preferred stocks are owned by a Subchapter C Corporation, 70% of the dividends they receive are excluded from federal income taxes, provided that the preferred stock is held for more than 45 days.

- **As credit plays**—Preferred stocks are junior level securities. As such, they generally have lower credit ratings than the more senior securities from the same issuer. The credit ratings of the junior level securities are also more volatile. If the credit quality of the company improves, the credit rating of the preferred stocks might be upgraded—resulting in some sudden price appreciation. Of course, if the company's credit quality declines, the credit quality of the preferred stock is often the first security to be downgraded.

CHAPTER TWELVE

Convertible Securities

A convertible security is a security that contains an embedded option that grants the investor the right to exchange the security for another type of security. While there are innumerable varieties of convertible securities, the most traditional and common types of convertible securities are bonds and preferred stocks that investors can exchange for a fixed number of shares of the company's common stock.

Consider a hypothetical bond issued by XYZ Inc. This bond is issued at par with a 6% coupon and includes an option that allows the bond to be converted at any time into 100 shares of a company's common stock. At the time the bond is issued, the company's common is selling for $8 per share and pays no dividend.

No rational investor would buy the bond and immediately exchange it for the stock since the $1,000 bond could only be exchanged for $800 (100 shares × $8 per share). However, if a year later the stock is selling for $16 per share, the bond can be converted into $1,600 worth of stock. If it was selling at any price below $1,600, an investor could make an immediate risk-free (arbitrage) profit by simultaneously buying the bond, exchanging it for stock, and selling the stock.

In reality, the bond would be worth more than $1,600 since, in addition to being convertible into $1,600 worth of the company's common, it generates $60 of income per year for the owner and is a more senior security. The present value of those future interest payments would have to be added to the conversion value in order to determine the bond's fair current market value.

CONVERSION VALUE

The conversion value is the current market value of the common stock into which the bond converts. It is calculated by multiplying the number of shares into which the bond converts by the current price of the common stock.

Conversion value = number of shares × price of the shares

In the example presented in the last section, the initial conversion value would be:

Conversion value = 100 × $8 = $800

After the stock rose to $16 per share, the conversion value would be:

Conversion value = 100 × $16 = $1,600

CONVERSION PREMIUM

The conversion premium is the difference between the market value and the conversion value of the bond—expressed on either an absolute or a percentage basis. In the XYZ Inc. example, the initial conversion premiums would be:

Absolute premium = $1,000 − $800 = $200
Percentage premium = ($1,000 − $800) / $800 = 25%

In the United States, the typical initial conversion premium for convertible bonds ranges from 10% to 30%. The greater the perceived upside potential of the stock, and the longer the period of call protection, the higher the conversion premium. If the bond is trading above its call price, then, as the bond approaches its call date, the conversion premium contracts. It contracts because, if the bond is called, the investor has to exchange the bond for the stock in order to avoid having it called. When the bond is exchanged, any conversion premium is lost.

WORK-OUT PERIOD

One of the most useful ratios for analysis of convertible bonds is the work-out period. The work-out period is a measure of how long it takes for the conversion premium to be amortized by the higher current income generated by the bond. In the XYZ Inc. example, the bond generates current income of $60 per year while the stock generates no income since it pays no dividends. Since the bond has a $200 conversion premium, the work-out period would be:

Work-out period = Conversion premium in dollars /
(income from bond − income from an equivalent
investment in stock)
Work-out period = $200 / ($60 − $0) = 3.33 years

If the stock generated a $0.10 dividend per year, then the work-out period would be:

Work-out period = $200 / ($60 − $12.50) = 4.21 years

Note that in this example, the income from the stock is $12.50 since $1,000 would buy 125 shares of stock at $8 each. In order to have a fair comparison, it is necessary to compute the work-out period using the income from an equal investment in both the convertible bond and the underlying common.

The shorter the work-out period, the more attractive the convertible is when compared to the underlying stock. Conservative investors are often willing to buy convertibles with work-out periods as long as 3.5 years, while aggressive investors are often unwilling to accept work-out periods longer than 2.5 years.

Why Do Investors Buy Convertible Securities?

Investors always have to choose between the various ways to invest in a company. They can invest directly by buying the common stock—or indirectly by buying a security that converts into the common. Convertibles offer investors numerous advantages relative to investing directly in common stock. Some of these advantages are listed below and include:

- **More senior security**—In the event the company files for bankruptcy, the investors who own the convertible bonds become creditors of the company and, as such, have a senior claim on any remaining assets relative to both the common and preferred holders. Of course, in order for this seniority to have any value, the company has to have assets after the more senior creditors, including the government, employees, and senior debt holders, are all paid in full.

- **Higher current income**—Convertible bonds almost always offer a higher current income than the underlying common stocks. The cash flow from the bond's interest payments almost always exceeds the dividend payments from an equal size investment in the underlying common stock. For investors that require or desire current income, convertibles are often the more attractive investment alternative.

- **Favorable risk adjusted return**—Because of the way that the value of the embedded conversion option changes as the price of the underlying instrument changes, the price of the convertible rises by more when the price of the underlying stock rises than the price of the convertible declines when the underlying stock declines. Thus, convertible securities exhibit a positive asymmetric risk-reward pattern in response to a change in the value of the underlying common.

- **Automatic tactical asset allocation**—One of the most attractive advantages of convertible securities is that they automate one of the most basic and important tactical asset allocation decisions investors have to decide, the decision of how much to allocate to equity versus fixed income. Many market timers try to increase the weighting of stocks in their portfolio when the market is rising, and retreat to the higher income and relative safety of bonds when they expect the stock market to decline. Fortunately, for owners of convertible securities, these securities behave more like stocks when the market is rising—and more like bonds when the market is either flat or declining. In effect, they automatically tactically reallocate in a way that benefits the investor.

What Are the Disadvantages of Convertible Securities?

While convertible securities offer numerous advantages, they also have some disadvantages that investors need to consider:

- **Underperforming the common**—In a down, flat, or slowly rising market, convertible securities outperform the underlying common. However, in a rapidly rising market, convertible securities underperform the stocks into which they convert.
- **Call risk**—Almost every convertible bond is callable. Generally, the bonds are callable either after a certain period of call protection is passed or after the stock price has risen to the point where the conversion option is deeply in the money. When the issuer calls the bond, the investor can lose any remaining conversion premium. Consider the following example:

   Suppose the XYZ Inc. bond introduced earlier in this chapter is purchased as a new issue and that subsequently the underlying stock price rises to $16 a share. Since the conversion value is $1,600 and the bond generates a higher current income, an investor might be willing to pay a $150 premium per bond over conversion value, $1,750 in this example. The extra $150 is the present value of the $60 annual payments.

   However, paying a premium over conversion value can be a disaster if the bond shortly becomes callable. If the bond is called at par (or par plus a small conversion premium), the investor would have little choice other than to convert the bond into the underlying common. Converting the bond that the investor paid $1,750 for into $1,600 worth of stock still beats accepting $1,000 (or $1,030) in cash.

When the bond is called, the $150 conversion premium ($1,750 – $1,600) is lost. Therefore, it is important for investors to research the call provisions of convertible securities prior to purchasing a convertible bond or a preferred. Investors should not pay a conversion premium that is higher than the present value of the incremental cash flows the investor can expect to receive from the bond before the bond is called.

- **Loss of accrued interest upon forced conversion**—When a convertible bond is called, and the investor is effectively forced to convert the bond into the underlying common in order to avoid receiving the call price for the bond, the investor also sacrifices any interest that the bond has accrued. Because they don't have to pay the accrued interest on bonds that are converted, many companies that have issued convertibles often force conversion by calling the securities just prior to an interest payment date.

  Thus, in a forced call an investor can lose both the conversion premium and any accrued interest. Because accrued interest is lost when a convertible is called, it is not uncommon for bonds that are likely to be called to be trading at a price that is equal to their conversion value minus their accrued interest.

- **Lower liquidity of convertibles**—Convertible securities have lower liquidity than the underlying common. Investors should use limit orders and build orders over time in order to avoid disturbing the market.

Why Do Issuers Issue Convertible Securities?

There are two main reasons why issuers elect to issue convertibles: to borrow money at a lower rate and/or to delay the issuance of stock in the hope that the stock can be issued in the future at a higher price.

By embedding a conversion option into its debt, companies with high credit ratings can borrow money at a lower interest rate than they would ordinarily have to pay. For start-up companies, or companies with low credit ratings, embedding a conversion option into its bond may be a necessary incentive to attract lenders even if the bonds offer a high return.

When companies issue convertibles, they hope that the bonds will eventually be converted into stock. If the conversion occurs, it will occur at a price that is higher than the stock's current price.

CHAPTER THIRTEEN

Behavioral Finance

Time and again emotion moves the markets more than rational analysis.

—J. P. MORGAN

Behavioral finance is often referred to as "the other side of investing." Investors select stocks based on fundamental, technical, and quantitative analysis. They select bonds based on credit and tax analysis. While these types of analysis are essential, they are not sufficient for investors to maximize the probability of success. There is another often overlooked component of investment success—namely, behavioral patterns. Some investors naturally exhibit behavior patterns that are either beneficial or detrimental to the investment performance of their portfolios.

Like artistic or athletic ability, being a successful investor has a certain genetic component. While we can all learn to:

- Play the violin, few of us will ever play at Carnegie Hall
- Do math, few of us will earn a Nobel Prize for contributing to the science
- Shoot a basketball, few of us will make a living in the NBA

Likewise, while we all can all become better investors, few of us will become the next Warren Buffett, John Templeton, Peter Lynch, or Ben Graham. Most of us have brains that simply aren't wired to be great. What's worse, some of us have brains that are wired in such a way that we are our own worst enemies when it comes to investing.

Just to be clear, we are not talking about intelligence. Some very bright people exhibit negative behavior patterns. They outsmart and outthink themselves. On the other hand, people with average or even below average intelligence can be great investors. The theory behind most equity strategies is fairly easy to understand. The hard part is having the discipline to execute the strategies correctly.

By identifying these destructive behaviors in ourselves, we can employ the following strategies:

- Adopt investment strategies and vehicles that mitigate the negative impact of our destructive behaviors.
- Recognize when our actions are mistakes, and avoid repeating them.
- Improve the risk-reward ratios of our portfolios.

Let's look at some of the negative behaviors and how they negatively impact investment performance.

TAKING LOSSES PERSONALLY

No investor, not even investors as good as Warren Buffett and John Templeton, wins 100% of the time. No matter how thoroughly a stock or a commodity market is researched, unexpected events can cause substantial losses. Dealing with losses in a professional and mature manner is a necessary part of being a successful investor. Unfortunately, not all investors deal with losses well. Instead, they take them personally. Now, of course, for the typical investor, there was nothing personal about Enron's fraud or the leakage of BP's gulf well—but some investors can't perceive them as just as unfortunate random events. When they take an unexpected loss, they exhibit one of two negative behaviors.

The first negative behavior is the "snake bit effect." Suppose you are seeking high income and, for the first time, you buy a high income REIT. Shortly thereafter, the REIT's dividend is cut because the vacancy rates rise unexpectedly. While it is appropriate for you to be disappointed—it's not appropriate to say, "I'll never buy a REIT again." If one bad experience causes you to permanently swear off investing in an entire asset class, you suffer from the "snake bit effect" and took the loss too personally.

The second negative behavior is a "rush to get even." When you take a loss, you irrationally feel cheated and "rush to get even." You indulge your rush by investing in progressively higher-risk investments. You lose money in a REIT and reinvest the proceeds in a risky stock. If the risky stock also proves to be a loser, you then want to trade options with the sale proceeds.

If you have a tendency toward these negative behaviors, adjust your investment strategy to reduce the number of potential "triggers." For example, seeking the next great growth stock requires taking a large number of losses and would be inappropriate for someone who takes loses personally. Instead, implement a dividend capture or option overwrite strategy.

Anchor Points

An anchor point is a meaningless number to which some people nevertheless attach great significance. For example, suppose you're walking past a store and you see a beautiful coat in the window. You enter the store, try on the coat, and not only does it fit perfectly—but you look in the mirror and the coat is very flattering. Now comes the moment of truth. You reach in the side packet and pull out the price tag and what you see is: $2,000 crossed out, $1,600 crossed out, $1,200 crossed out, $1,000 crossed out, $750 "final reduction"—does this make you more likely to buy the coat? For most people the answer is "yes." For some, the proposition is irresistible! They believe they are getting a bargain—a $2,000 coat for $750. The $2,000 is an anchor point. The clerk just wrote the progressively lower prices on the tag and crossed them out to make the buyer believe he or she was getting a great deal.

As another example, the talking heads on TV-market programs will pontificate for weeks about whether and when the S&P 500 will break 1,500 or 2,000. What's so special about 1,500 as opposed to 1,499 or 1,501? The answer is nothing—other than it's a round number. What's special about a round number? Nothing! Yet, great baggage is attached to this meaningless number.

Studies have shown that suggesting a value (either high or low) to real estate appraisers before they do their work will significantly impact their valuations.

As another example, De Beers ran a great advertising campaign in which they planted an anchor point: "Tell her you love her with two months' salary." Now, when young men walk into a jewelry store this anchor point is in the back of their mind when they are asked, "And how much do you want to spend?"

If you find yourself thinking any of the following you have a sensitivity to anchor points:

- *"I'll buy the stock when it hits $20 because that's where I made money last time."* Last time could have been two years ago in a different market with a different management team and a different business environment. In others words, the $20 past price could be too high or too low and is today an irrelevant anchor point.

- *"I'll sell when I get even."* Delaying a sale just to avoid taking a loss exhibits two negative behaviors: Sales resistance and anchor points. If it is appropriate to sell—do so, and redeploy the capital to something more promising.
- *"I'll sell when it doubles."* What's so special about a double? If you have the right stock at the right time it can appreciate 4 to 100 times. Great stocks are hard to find; when you find one, why settle for a double?
- *"The stock's cheap because it's well below its previous high."* Just because it is well below its previous high doesn't make it cheap.

Differential Valuation of Money

This may seem to be an obvious statement: "The value of every US dollar is the same." Surprisingly, however, a large portion of the population doesn't see it that way. Instead, the perceived value of a dollar is influenced by its source, shape, and payment size.

For example, when people are asked are they more likely to buy something frivolous with money coming from work or gambling earnings, they reply they are far more likely to spend gambling winnings on something frivolous. Clearly, they don't put equal value on the dollars because of their source. Likewise, when asked about money from work or gifts, the answer is the same. Gifted dollars are less highly valued. Thus, the source of the money matters. The Ferrari dealer at Wynn in Las Vegas sells more Ferraris than all the other Ferrari dealers worldwide combined—and the dealer doesn't even allow test drives!

Ask yourself this question: "You walk into the casino with $200 for a night of fun. You run it up to $500. Then you lose it all. How much did you lose?" Some people will say $500. Others will say $200. Those that say $200 have a problem. In their minds the other $300 is the "house's money" and they tend to be more free with how they bet it or spend it. If you can leave the casino with the $500 and the guard doesn't shoot you—it is your money. If, at any point, you were up to $500 but left empty-handed—you lost $500.

The shape also matters. More people are likely to spend (over-spend?) when they pay with a charge card than cash. This is the entire basis of the card industry and is why merchants are willing to pay 1.5% to 3.5% of the sale to the card company. Gamblers will bet more when using chips than with cash currency. Fine resorts just ask patrons to sign for drinks, massages, boat rentals, and the like—no "messy money" until checkout time.

The size of incoming and outgoing payments also impacts their value. Small increases in cash flows are often wasted. Someone who receives an extra $20 a day is most likely to be spend it. However, present the same amount in one lump sum at the end of the year in a check for $5,000—and then it becomes "real money" that starts a serious kitchen table conversation. "Maybe we should put it in the kid's college fund, or an IRA." On the spending side, every sales person knows that to sell that $600 phone with the 2-year contract you say, "It is less than a $1 a day" or "It costs less than a cup of coffee a day" in an attempt to lower its perceived cost.

From your perspective, be on the lookout for the following tells that you have a problem with money:

- Do you frequently regret making purchases on your charge card?
- If you received a sudden unexpected $10,000 inheritance, how likely would you be to use it for something extravagant (vacation, jewelry, adding a sauna room) that you wouldn't buy normally?

- Positive answers to either questions show a propensity for this negative behavior.

Publicity Bias

Stocks in the news tend to have lower returns than less well-known companies. When most investors do a search to identify stocks that meet their desired criteria they might enter something like: $1B–$10B market cap, >200K average daily trading volume, >3% dividend, 3 years dividend increases, P/E <25. As additional sorting criteria are added, the number of companies that meet all of the criteria declines. Once the list of possible investments gets whittled down to eight to ten names, the investor then has to select one or more. The tendency is to select the best known name. As a result, the best known companies trade at the highest relative price—and, therefore, often offer the lowest relative return.

Look at your portfolio. Are all the stocks household names? If so, you may suffer from publicity bias. If you do suffer from this bias, then you need to make a conscious effort to widen your horizons.

Interpretation Bias

When reading research reports, newspapers, newsletters, proxy statements, and/or market analysis, investors tend to focus on, spend more time on, and give more credence to, points that support their existing opinion—regardless of whether that position is bullish or bearish.

The human brain craves positive reinforcement:

- "How do I look in this dress?"
- "How did I come across at the meeting?"
- "Do my new glasses make me look trendy?"
- "How did you think my proposal sounded?"

When a university created a perfectly balanced research report, meaning that it contained equal:

- Number of positive and negative points
- Wordage for the positive and negative points
- Power in the words used in both the positive and negative points

the report was shown to investors who were "long" the stock and to those who were "short" the stock. Not surprisingly, they both thought that, on balance, the research report supported their existing position. Investors also make a conscious effort to seek out and focus on alternative viewpoints. You need to seek out alternate opinions even though they are unpleasant to read. The last thing a "gold bug" needs to do is live on the gold bug sites. Someone who is "long gold" needs to focus on the contrary opinion to learn something new.

Overconfidence

As a species, humans are overly confident and overly optimistic.

- Ask a roomful of people which of you are "below average" drivers. Less than 5% will put up their hands even though, by definition, 50% of the attendees must be below average.
- Find a group of people who do not know what their IQ score is, explain the scoring system (100 is average, 140 is genius, etc.) and ask people to rank themselves; most people will give themselves 10 to 15 points over their true IQ.
- To see true "mass delusion," ask a group of middle-aged men to rate their athletic ability.

This tendency toward overconfidence crosses all ethnic, class, wealth, and education barriers. For example, the management team at Long Term Capital Management, which included two Nobel Prize winners and state-of-the-art technology, was grossly overly optimistic about its ability to manage risk. Both ditch diggers and world-class programmers frequently underestimate the time to complete a project. Investors who suffer from overconfidence exhibit three behaviors:

- They expect to earn a rate of return higher than market average, despite having no real competitive advantage over their competitors.
- They have portfolios that are underdiversified, since they are sure their stocks will outperform.
- They trade excessively because they believe they can predict short-term price movements.

The groups that most often exhibit overconfidence are, in order:

- Single men
- Married women
- Single women
- Married men

There's a lesson in there somewhere!

Pain When Selling

Buying new stocks is easy. When investors buy new stocks to add to their portfolios, the investors have already concluded that the new stocks are the "fairest of them all" and so are full of optimism. An analogy would be buying a stock is like going on a highly anticipated first date: the investor is hoping all sorts of great things are going to happen.

Selling a stock, however, is more complex. It turns out that it is not just hoarders who have trouble selling. Investors often experience pain when selling:

- If the stock is sold at a loss the investor must admit that buying it was a mistake. Some investors have trouble admitting mistakes. This is the divorce sale.
- If the stock has been a winner, it creates feelings of loyalty. They say, "The stock's been good to me." Now, of course, a stock can't be good or bad and doesn't know the investor's alive, but some people attribute stocks with living characteristics.
- It can be especially painful for an investor to sell the stock of a company for which the investor worked. This is especially true if the investor enjoyed working at the company and had an extended career with the company. The happier the employee and the longer the employee's career, the greater the pain of selling the stock. For some, it is like retiring all over again. For many, retiring is very stressful—separating from friends and a familiar routine, losing a sense of purpose, and acknowledging that time is marching on. Selling the employer's stock brings up all of these negative feelings all over again. Some investors' entire portfolio is nearly one stock—the stock of their former employer.

The result of over-optimism is that investors want to sell winners too soon and losers too late. If you suffer from this negative behavior, enter stop loss and limit sell orders with each stock purchase. This way the sell decisions are predetermined.

Confusing Information with Knowledge

Many investors confuse information (data) with knowledge (ability to analyze data to make predictions). For example, suppose you are in Vegas and the last six rolls of the roulette wheel all landed on black. Would you bet red or black for the next roll? Intellectually, we know each roll is an independent event and that the past rolls have no bearing on future rules; however, some gamblers will *feel* that:

- Red is "due" and will bet red
- Black has set a trend and bet on the trend continuing

In their minds, the past results have somehow changed the odds of the next roll—even though they know the wheel hasn't changed.

Thus, knowing the past results is data—but analyzing the data conveys no knowledge.

To see if you suffer from this behavior, which of the below series of coin flips is more likely:

- HTHTHTHT
- HHHHHHHH

Of course, they are both equally likely, but you'll be surprised how many otherwise savvy people will pick the first one.

Investors who confuse information with knowledge often place undue trust in technical and/or quantitative analysis.

Social Pressure

It's not just teenage girls who suffer from social pressure. Investors suffer from social pressure as well. Imagine a Saturday morning in a modestly upscale suburban neighborhood. At 10 a.m. the lawnmowers start and, by 12:30, the clippings are collected and the neighbors congregate in someone's backyard. A cooler of beer appears, and the neighbors start chatting about what neighbors in many neighborhoods chat about:

- How does the high school football team look this year?
- How is the new police chief working out?
- Are property taxes going up this year?

Then, the conversation gets around to investing:

- One neighbor talks about a new search-agent company he found whose algorithm is so good—it is going to make Google cry. Everyone else asks a bunch of questions.
- The next talks about a biotech company that came up with a serum that dissolves the plaque that forms in heart arteries, and how it is going to make most heart surgery obsolete. Everyone else asks a bunch of questions.
- Another neighbor talks about a seed company that created a seed that is self-fertilizing and requires only one-tenth of the water of a traditional plant. Everyone else asks a bunch of questions.
- The conversation comes around to you, and you say "I own an S&P 500 index fund." The investment may be appropriate for you—but you are going to feel left out because no one is going to ask any questions.

Let's go upmarket to a cocktail party/fundraiser on 82nd Street and 3rd Avenue in New York City. You are milling about, and the conversation starts about hedge funds. Each person in order talks about the hedge fund(s) they are in and the exotic strategies they are pursuing. The conversation gets around to you and you proudly state

"I own an S&P 500 index fund on 30% leverage." Sixty seconds later you are standing in the corner by yourself, thinking "I better get a hedge fund."

Just like fashion, investments have trends. Those who don't follow the trend can feel left out and start making investments for the wrong reasons.

Conclusion

In order to successfully manage your portfolio, not only do you need to understand portfolio theory and investments, you also need to know yourself. Track your transactions and look for soft issues that are self-destructive and try to eliminate them.

CHAPTER FOURTEEN

Trading Securities

Security transactions take place either on an exchange or in the OTC market. While the purpose of both the exchanges and the OTC market is to match securities buyers and sellers, the way they operate can be very different. For example, the mechanics of how stocks on the New York Stock Exchange (NYSE) execute transactions is very different than those on the NASDAQ Exchange.

How a Trade Is Executed on an Exchange

The NYSE

When a customer wants to buy or sell a stock that trades on the NYSE, he or she places an order with a firm that is a member of the exchange. Only firms that are members of the exchange can transact business there. Being a member of an exchange is referred to having a "seat" on that exchange. Operationally, member firms have order rooms around the perimeter of the exchange to get their customers' orders into the market.

A customer's order is transmitted electronically to the firm's order booth. The order booth then relays the order to a floor broker, who in turn directs that order to the specific location where that stock trades. It is important to note that each stock on the exchange trades in a specific location. That location is determined by the Direct Market Maker (DMM). Historically, these DMMs were referred to as *specialists*. The order can then be executed either with a floor broker from another firm or with the DMM. The role of the DMM is to provide liquidity and maintain an orderly market in that stock. Therefore, if no one else is available to buy or sell that security, the DMM must perform that function. The DMM also acts as an auctioneer in an open outcry auction market environment to bring buyers and sellers together and to manage the actual auction. On occasion, they facilitate the liquidity in a stock by committing their own capital to buy and sell that security. Of particular note, the DMM is neither an employee of the company whose stock they handle nor of the exchange. Once the order is executed, a report is sent back to the firm's order room to inform the client that the transaction was completed.

It was only in 1995 that the process described above was automated. For the first 203 years of its existence, the NYSE was a paper-based market. The transmission of the order to the broker or DMM occurred when the order room on the floor generated a paper ticket, which had to be "run" by the broker to the trading post for that stock. By 2007, all NYSE orders could be transmitted electronically to both the broker and the specialist.

The NASDAQ System

The NASDAQ market was created by the National Association of Securities Dealers (NASD) in 1971, as a way of providing liquidity in securities that did not trade on recognized exchanges. Originally, it was an example of the OTC market. At that time, it was the world's first electronic trading platform. Over the years, it has grown into much more, but it was not until 2006 that NASDAQ (National Association of Securities Dealers Automated Quotations) evolved from a technology-based trading platform (stock market) to a licensed, recognized national exchange.

Highlights of NASDAQ's evolution include:

- In 1992, it joined with the London Stock Exchange to form the first intercontinental linkage of securities markets.
- In 2000, NASDAQ was spun off from the regulatory authority NASD (National Association of Securities Dealers) to form a publicly traded company, the NASDAQ Stock Market Inc.
- In 2006, NASDAQ changed from stock market to licensed national exchange.
- In 2007, NASDAQ bought the Philadelphia Stock Exchange (PHLX). First established in 1790, PHLX is the oldest stock exchange in America.

Dealer firms (market makers) that wish to buy and sell securities can post their bids and offers electronically. Because the system is computerized, market makers can change their bids and offers throughout the day as market conditions change.

Because subscribers use this information for different purposes, not all subscribers need access to the same level of information. For this reason, NASDAQ offers different levels of service, representing various levels of complexity and, of course, cost:

- **Level One**—This level shows only the highest bid price and the lowest offer price for a given security, without disclosing the name of the market-making firm providing that price. This disclosure, of the highest bid and offer, is called the *inside market*.
- **Level Two**—Service at this level shows what every participating market-making firm is bidding and offering for every NASDAQ listed security. This indicates not only the inside market but other firms' prices, as well. This information can tell traders which firms are interested in buying or selling that security and at what price.
- **Level Three**—This level is available to only market-maker firms. It allows the traders to enter, delete, or update quotations for securities in which they are the market maker.

MARKET MAKERS

The liquidity of the NASDAQ market is provided by market makers. These firms buy and sell securities for their own account. Before a firm can "make a market" in a security, it has to meet certain qualifications relating to its net capital. The department that decides which securities it wants to be a market maker in, and what those prices will be, is called the trading department. Each trader is assigned certain securities to trade. For example, one trader may be assigned XYZ security, and because of the volume of trades in that security, that may be the only security they trade. Other traders may cover more than one security, due to their more limited volume or liquidity. Traders are usually clustered by industry. For example, traders in pharmaceutical stocks will usually be physically situated together, as will banking and finance traders, manufacturing, technology, and so forth, to facilitate the flow of information.

The price at which a firm stands ready to buy a security is called the bid price. The price at which the firm stands ready to sell a security is called the offer (or ask) price. By being willing to both buy and sell a given security, a firm "makes a market" in the security. As market conditions change during the day, the trader raises or lowers the firm's bid and offer prices. By standing ready to buy and sell securities at the posted prices, these traders play the same role the DMMs do on the exchange floor. The factors that influence where a trader is willing to make a market in a particular security are both quantitative and qualitative. They can include:

- **Customer order flow**—If the firm's clients are selling securities, the firm might lower its bid accordingly, so as to not pay too much for that security. If the clients are buyers, the firm might raise the price to meet this growing demand.
- **Research**—Based on fundamental, technical, or quantitative analysis, the firm or the trader might have a conviction on the price of the security, and would trade the security for their account accordingly.
- **Capital**—If a firm already has a substantial amount of capital committed to a particular position, the firm might adjust its price to reduce those capital needs.

THE OVER-THE-COUNTER MARKET

Any security transaction that does not take place on a securities exchange is said to occur in the OTC market. Items usually traded in the OTC market here in the United States include:

- US government securities
- US agency securities
- Corporate bonds
- Municipal bonds
- Mortgage backed and asset backed bonds
- Options (stock, bond, currency)
- Warrants
- American depository receipts (ADRs)

Many investors are initially confused by the OTC market because it has no central location, unlike a traditional exchange with its centralized trading floor. Instead, the OTC market is a telecommunications market. It consists of dealer firms located throughout the country, any of which can trade with the other. Since phone communication can reach virtually anywhere, the OTC market is said to be a market without geographic or physical boundaries.

Brokers and Dealers

In any one OTC transaction, a firm can act as either a broker or a dealer. When a firm takes an order from a client, and then merely executes that order, it is said to be acting as the client's agent, or broker. In this type of transaction, the firm never owns the security, but merely performs an order execution service for the client.

When a firm buys securities from its clients (using its own money) or sells securities to its clients out of its own inventory, it is acting as a principal, or dealer. In these transactions, the firm itself is on the other side of the client's trade, acting as the counterparty. When acting as a dealer, the firm is putting its own capital at risk.

Most firms act in both capacities at different times. They act as brokers when their clients want to buy or sell securities that the firms do not have in their inventory or that are traded on an exchange. They act as dealers when their clients want to sell securities that the firm itself wants to buy or when the clients want to buy securities the firms already have in inventory. Firms that are licensed to act in both capacities are called broker/dealer firms, and fall under the regulatory authority of FINRA (Financial Industry Regulatory Authority).

The broker/dealers compensation depends on the function they are performing in the transaction. When acting as agent, the brokerage firm charges its customers a commission to perform that function. When acting as a principal, the firm does not charge a commission, but rather:

- Tries to buy the securities for less than the price at which they can be resold.
- Tries to sell the security at a price greater than what they paid for it.

This price differential is called many different names: markup, spread, P/L. Sometimes, the firms are successful at making a profit on principal trades, sometimes they are not.

Example: Dependable Brokerage Inc. gets three orders from its clients in a given morning.

- The first order is to sell 2,000 shares of an exchange-listed security. They first send the order to the floor of the exchange, where it is executed at the best possible price for its client. For its services, the firm charges the client a commission.
- The second order is to buy 500 shares of a stock that is traded OTC. The firm itself does not have any of this security in its own inventory, so it has to buy the stock on the client's behalf from another firm. The firm contacts a number of firms that have the stock in their inventory to see which firm will sell it

for the lowest price. After finding the lowest price, the firm buys the 500 shares, and bills the client for the purchase price plus a commission. The firm acted as its client's agent, but this time in the OTC market.

- The third order is from a client who wants to buy 3,000 shares of a different OTC security. The firm has this security in its own inventory, so it becomes the seller, and fills the client's buy order. Because the firm acts as a principal in the transaction, it cannot charge the client a commission. Instead, the firm "marks up" or raises the price it charges for the securities. If the firm bought these 3,000 shares for less than the price at which it sells them to the client, the firm makes a profit on the transaction. If, however, the firm bought the shares at a higher price than the price at which it sells the shares to the client, it incurs a loss on the transaction.

MARKET MAKING

When a firm buys and sells securities for its own account, it is said to be market making. Before a firm can "make a market" in a security, it has to meet certain requirements relating to its net capital, as detailed in FINRA regulations. These regulations are designed to make sure that a firm has enough capital to back up its quotes so that there is little credit risk in the market.

Each trader within a firm is assigned certain securities to trade. For example, one trader may be responsible for trading OTC oil stocks, while another may be responsible for trading OTC computer stocks. Every minute of every day that the market is open, these traders decide:

- What prices their firms will pay to buy the securities that they trade.

- The prices at which their firms stand ready to sell the securities that they trade.

These traders play the same role that the specialists and direct market makers do on the exchange floor.

Example: A trader at Dependable Brokerage Inc. is responsible for making a market in OTC computer stocks. For one of these companies, Wizz Bang Computers Inc. (WBCI), the trader is currently making the market:

29.75 by 30

In other words, the firm stands ready to buy WBCI at $29.75 and to sell it for $30. Note that the price at which the firm stands ready to sell the stock is $0.25 higher than the price at which it will buy it. This $0.25 difference, called the spread, is how the firm makes a profit. By buying the stock for $0.25 less than it sells the stock for, the firm makes a profit of a quarter on every share it buys then resells.

So, if the price stays constant throughout the day and the trader buys 5,000 shares and sells 5,000 shares, the firm makes a profit of $0.25 × 5,000, or $1,250.

Unfortunately for the brokerage firms and their traders, trading is not quite so easy. Ideally, traders would like to buy and sell the same number of shares each and every day, so that, at day's end, they would not have any inventory to be worried about overnight. If the traders are getting more buyers than sellers (that is, having more people buy from they than are selling to them), they compensate by raising the bid and ask prices.

Example: The trader was making a market 29.75 by 30. Now, getting more buyers, she might change her market to:

30 by 30.25

In other words, the trader is now willing to pay $30 per share and willing to sell it for $30.25 a share. By raising the bid price (increasing the price she is willing to pay), the trader hopes to attract more sellers. By raising the offer price (increasing the price at which she is willing to sell), the trader hopes to attract fewer buyers. By attracting more sellers and fewer buyers, the trader hopes to bring the number of buy and sell orders back into balance. Maintaining balance is important so that the traders do not get caught with a lot of inventory in a bad market.

Example: While making a market in WBCI at 30 by 30.25, the trader receives more sell orders (totaling 10,000 shares) than buy orders (totaling 5,000 shares). By the middle of the trading day, the firm owns 5,000 shares of WBCI. If the market suddenly drops, or if negative news about WBCI should be announced, the most anyone might be willing to pay for WBCI is, say, $28. In such a case, the market for WBCI falls to 28 by 28.25 and the firm has a loss of $10,000 ($2 per share × 5,000 shares).

The same situation results when the price of the stock moves up sharply after the trader shorts the stock. (Many traders sell stock short, to fill buy orders if they do not have any shares in their inventory. They then hope to buy the shares at their lower bid price to cover the short position and make a profit.)

So, traders who do not want to speculate with the firm's capital always try to adjust their bid and offer prices so that they are buying and selling approximately the same number of shares at all times. Traders are generally not hurt by sharp rising or falling markets unless they build up a substantial long or short position in that security. If they are willing to settle for a small profit on each transaction, little market risk is involved.

But why settle for a small profit? If the firm profits by buying low and selling high, why not widen the spread? For example, instead of bidding 29.75 for WBCI and offering at 30, why not bid 28 and offer to sell at 34? The firm would then make $6 on every share it bought and sold.

Widening the spread for greater profit is not feasible for several reasons.

First, FINRA has a 5 percent guideline that prohibits price differentials of more than 5 percent, except under extraordinary circumstances. Only if the firm incurs any extraordinary expense in trying to fill a client's order can it exceed the 5 percent guideline.

Second, the competition among dealers for each other's business and the client's business is fierce. Very often a number of firms all make markets in the same securities. Anyone who wants to buy the security—either other firms or clients—of course, will buy it from the firm offering it at the lowest price. Likewise, and firm or client wanting to sell the security will sell it to the firm willing to pay the highest price for it. Thus, a firm that posts low bids or high offers will just not do any business.

Posting Quotes

How do firms make their prices known to other dealers and clients? The answer depends on the security itself and the amount of capital that issuing company has.

The Pink Sheets

If the issuing company is small or the security is rarely traded, the security is listed in the National Quotation Bureau (NQB) sheets. These daily sheets list the securities currently being offered for sale or sought after for purchase, and the firms (with their phone number) trying to sell them.

The sheets that contain the stock and warrant listings are called the pink sheets because they were historically printed on pink paper. Today, they are available through many information providers as a data feed. On any given day, the listing contains about 11,000 different OTC stocks and warrants. The sheets/data feed that contain the corporate bond listings are called the yellow sheet, because historically they were printed on yellow paper.

Because these sheets are not updated minute-by-minute, yet the value of these securities can change constantly, a prospective buyer or seller of the securities listed in the pink sheets must call the firms listed in the sheets and get their most current bids or offers. Firms that indicate an interest in buying or selling these securities by posting prices in the pink sheets are said to have "an ax to grind."

Types of Quotations

Security dealers, particularly those who deal primarily in thinly traded securities, can make or obtain several quotes: firm, subject, and work-out.

Firm Quotes

Firm bids or offers are prices at which the broker/dealer is committed to buy or sell a specific amount of a security. A firm bid or offer is usually good for the moment the quote is given, but it may also be firm for a longer period. Also, unless otherwise stated, it is good for at least one unit of trading. In other words, the broker's/dealer's commitment to buy or sell at the quoted price is limited to 100 shares of stock or 10 bonds at the quoted price. (Bond dealers vary greatly with regard to the size of the firm quotes.) Often, the broker/dealer will indicate not only the price, but how many shares or bonds they are willing trade at that price.

Subject Quotes

When a broker/dealer gives a quote and says it's "subject," then the quote is subject to confirmation. The broker/dealer needs more information before making the quote firm. Subject quotes can be expressed in several ways, including:

- "It's quoted 10–10.50."
- "Last I saw was 10–10.50."
- "It's 10–10.50 subject."

Work-Out Quotes

Sometimes, there is a very wide spread and the broker follows the quote with the word "work-out." This means the quote is not firm. It merely provides a range within which the broker/dealer believes a price can be "worked out." These quotes are most commonly used for infrequently traded securities.

ELECTRONIC COMMERCE NETWORKS

An electronic commerce network (ECN) is an automated trading system that allows investors to enter and execute orders in real time without the intervention of an intermediary, such as a broker. ECNs are technology driven, and have rapidly changed the way in which both retail and institutional trading is done. The rapid rise in technology, not only in the workplace, but also in the home, with the proliferation of personal computers, has fueled the growth of this new type of marketplace.

ECNs effectively began with the launch of the Reuters Group's Instinet, which is still one of the largest ECNs. Instinet began in 1969 as a system for investment managers to execute OTC transactions. Instinet allowed mutual funds and other institutional investors to post orders anonymously, at prices inside the wide spreads often found in NASDAQ stocks. ECNs can act as a broker or as a quasi-stock exchange. Until recently, the SEC's interpretation of the definition of an exchange reflected relatively rigid regulatory requirements and classifications for exchanges and broker/dealers. Advances in technology and the emergence of ECNs have increasingly blurred these distinctions. The statutory definition of exchange includes "a marketplace or facilities for bringing together purchasers and sellers of securities or otherwise performing, with respect to securities, the functions commonly performed by a stock exchange." With ECNs, the natural economic distinctions between stock exchanges and broker/dealers have been broken down. Exchanges and brokers are now doing the same thing.

Advantages of ECNs include cost reduction, faster execution, anonymous trading, and extended trading hours (often referred to as "after-hours trading"). The best prices are simply determined by the most aggressive order to buy (the highest bid) and the most aggressive order to sell (the lowest offering). If an order is executed, buy and sell prices are transmitted to brokers and/or exchanges. If orders cannot be matched, they are routed to other ECNs or to other exchanges for execution.

The major differences between the traditional methods of trading and the way in which ECNs operate are in the process, trading time, the pricing mechanism, and economics. In the ECN market, bids and asked quotes are entered and maintained in computer systems, either directly by the investor or through their broker. When an order to either buy or sell is placed, it is automatically matched with the best available bid/ask quote and automatically executed. In the ECNs market, after-hours trading is available. This allows for liquidity in issues, even when the traditional exchanges are closed.

Further blurring the lines between exchanges, ECNs, and brokers, in 2005 NASDAQ bought Instinet and Island, two prominent firms in the ECN marketplace.

Dark Pools

Dark pools are an evolution of the ECN marketplace that allows institutional investors to trade large blocks of stock with greater anonymity and avoid impacting the market with their orders. Unlike the traditional ECNs, these trading platforms allow the participants to enter their orders anonymously, unaware of other large orders that might be in the marketplace. Traditional ECNs offer the investors transparency as the bids and offers on the ECNs are reflected to the public. By contrast, bids and offerings on the dark pools are not transparent to market participants. One of the main advantages for institutional investors to use dark pools is for buying or selling large blocks of securities without "tipping their hand" to others and, thereby, avoid affecting the stock price. This is because neither the size of the trade nor the identity are revealed until after the trade is filled. Trades that are executed via dark pools are reported to the consolidated tape. However, they are recorded as over-the-counter transactions. As a result, detailed information about the volumes and types of transactions is left to the crossing network to report to clients if required.

Regulatory Environment

Given both its incredible importance to the economy and the massive amount of money that flows through the securities market, effective regulation is essential. Regulators must maintain the integrity of the markets, protect investors against fraud, and yet let the markets operate as freely as possible.

FINRA

The FINRA was created in 2007 through the consolidation of the NASD, with the enforcement arm of the NYSE, NYSE Regulation Inc. FINRA was organized under the 1938 Maloney Act, an amendment (Section 15A) to the Securities and Exchange Act of 1934. Although supervised by the SEC, FINRA operates, not as a government agency, but as an independent, self-regulating organization (SRO). Much of FINRA's responsibility in regulating the securities industry incorporates aspects of the trading as well.

Purpose of FINRA

As the successor to the NASD, FINRA's objective is to protect America's investors by making sure the securities industry operates fairly and honestly. As of 2013, FINRA oversees approximately 4,270 brokerage firms and 630,345 registered securities representatives. According to their mission statement, "FINRA is dedicated to investor protection and market integrity through effective and efficient regulation of the securities industry."

FINRA's power to regulate lies in its ability to deny membership to any broker/dealers operating in an unethical or improper manner. Because only FINRA members have the advantage of price concessions, discounts, and similar allowances, the loss of membership privileges all but prevents a firm from competing in the marketplace. In addition, FINRA members are permitted to do business only with the other members, although they may deal with foreign banks and dealers.

How FINRA Is Organized

The FINRA bylaws provide that the FINRA board of governors must consist of the Chief Executive Officer of FINRA, the Chief Executive Officer of NYSE Regulation, ten Industry Governors, and eleven Public Governors, including a Floor Member Governor, an Investment Company Affiliate Governor, an Independent Dealer/Insurance Affiliate Governor, three Small Firm Governors, one Midsize Firm Governor, and three Large Firm Governors. The Small Firm Governors, Midsize Firm Governor, and Large Firm Governors are elected by members of FINRA based on their classification as a Small Firm, Midsize Firm, or Large Firm.

Trade Reporting and Compliance Engine

FINRA's commitment to "investor protection and market integrity" is well illustrated by their development of the Trade Reporting and Compliance Engine (TRACE) in 1998. Under current TRACE regulations, US broker/dealers are required to report transactions in all corporate bonds, and most mortgage-backed and asset-backed securities to FINRA within 15 minutes of executing the trade. FINRA then posts these transactions on their website, available for the public to see (FINRA.org). Traditionally, as an example of the OTC market, the bond market has not offered investors the opportunity to see what price particular securities are trading at, making the determination of a fair pricing more difficult. By requiring dealers to report these transactions, FINRA is trying to improve price transparency and fair pricing. Investors and market participants who are trading bonds use this data (both historical and potentially as recently as 15 minutes ago) to help determine how competitive the prices they are receiving on bond transactions are.

FINRA Rules of Fair Practice

The Rules of Fair Practice were established as part of the NASD by-laws, now adopted by FINRA. They promote and enforce the highest conduct for the securities industry. The most basic of the rules is Section 1, Article III, which states the fundamental philosophy of FINRA: "a member, in the conduct of his business, must observe high standards of commercial honor and just and equitable principles of trade."

The broad-based Rules of Fair Practice include specific areas of the securities business. Some of the areas addressed by the rules are discussed in the next sections.

FINRA Member Firm Advertising

The Rules of Fair Practice consider it a violation for a member to publish, circulate, or distribute an advertisement, sales literature, or market letter that a member knows to contain untrue, false, or misleading statements. Similarly, no material fact or qualification can be omitted from advertising material if such an omission causes the underlying material to be misleading. In short, all advertising, sales, and marketing literature must be based on the principles of fair dealing and good faith.

Execution of Retail Trades

To help assure that all customers may benefit from a free and open market, FINRA members must use "reasonable diligence"—that is, all pertinent factors—to make sure that the customer gets the best possible price under prevailing market conditions. The rules state that a member's obligations to do the best for customers is not fulfilled by channeling business through another broker/dealer, unless using a third party reduces costs to the customer.

Receipt and Delivery of Securities

No member may accept a customer's purchase or order for any security without first making sure that the customer agrees to receive those securities against payment. On the sell side, no member may sell securities for a customer without being reasonably sure that the customer possesses the securities and will deliver them within the three business day settlement.

Forwarding of Reports and Proxy Material

When securities are held for a customer by the brokerage firm, they are usually held in *street name* (that is, in the name of the broker/dealer). In these cases, the issuer of the security sends all literature, including reports and proxies (voting rights) to the brokerage firm, not the customer. If the FINRA members do not promptly forward such material to customers, their conduct can be regarded as inconsistent with high standards of commercial honor.

Recommendations to Customers

According to the Rules of Fair Practice, all recommendations to customers to purchase, sell, or exchange securities must be based on reasonable grounds and be suitable for the customer. The controlling factor is the best interest of the customer. To determine suitability, the member is expected to learn about the financial condition of the customer.

FINRA Uniform Practice Code

The Uniform Practice Code (UPC) was first established as part of the NASD bylaws, now adopted by FINRA. The purpose is to assure uniformity in the customs, practices, and trading technology among the FINRA members. The code includes rules for the trading terms, delivery, payment, computation of interest, and recourse procedures. Some of the highlights of the UPC include:

- **Delivery of Securities**—For each security transaction, there are two key dates: the trade date and the delivery date.
- **Trade Date**—The transaction takes place on the trade date. The FINRA code requires that all ordinary transactions be confirmed in writing on or before the first full day following the trade date.
- **Delivery Date**—The delivery date is the date on which payment is due. There are several types of delivery:
  - *Cash*—Settlement occurs on the same day as the trade itself. Cash settlement is used when the client has to settle a transaction before a certain date, such as year-end for tax purposes.
  - *Next day*—The transaction is settled the first business day after the trade date.
  - *Regular way*—The seller agrees to deliver the securities to the office of the buyer on the third full business day following the transaction date.
  - *Buyer's option*—This type of delivery gives the buyer the option to receive securities on a specific date.
  - *Seller's option*—For securities other than US government securities, this type of delivery allows the seller to have the securities at the buyer's office on or before the business day that the seller specifies. For example, if securities are sold "seller's 30," the seller can deliver up to 30 days from the trade date, as long as one day's notice is given and three business days have elapsed from the trade date. This type of delivery is often requested by sellers who have difficulty getting possession of the securities.

advice. You should not rely on statements or representations made within the book or by any externally referenced sources. If you need investment, tax, or legal advice upon which you intend to rely in the course of your financial, business, or legal affairs, consult a competent, independent financial advisor, accountant, or attorney.

The contents of this book should not be taken as financial or legal advice, or as an offer to buy or sell any securities, fund, type of fund, or financial instruments. It should not be taken as an endorsement or recommendation of any particular company or individual, and no responsibility can be taken for inaccuracies, omissions, or errors. The information presented is not to be considered investment or legal advice. The reader should consult a Registered Investment Advisor or registered dealer or attorney prior to making any investment or legal decision.

The author does not assume any responsibility for actions or nonactions taken by people who have read this book, and no one shall be entitled to a claim for detrimental reliance based upon any information provided or expressed herein. Your use of any information provided herein does not constitute any type of contractual relationship between yourself and the provider(s) of this information. The author hereby disclaims all responsibility and liability for all use of any information provided in this book.

The materials here are not to be interpreted as establishing an attorney-client or any other relationship between the reader and the author or his firm.

Although great effort has been expended to ensure that only the most meaningful resources are referenced in these pages, the author does not endorse, guarantee, or warranty the accuracy, reliability, or thoroughness of any referenced information, product, or service. Any opinions, advice, statements, services, offers, or other information or content expressed or made available by third parties are those of the author(s) or publisher(s) alone. Reference to other sources of information does not constitute a referral, endorsement, or recommendation of any product or service. The existence of any particular reference is simply intended to imply potential interest to the reader.

The views expressed herein are exclusively those of the author and do not represent the views of any other person or any organization with which the author is, or may be, associated.

INDEX

Page numbers in **bold** indicate tables; those in *italic* indicate figures.

ABOUT THE AUTHOR

Stuart Veale is the president and founder of the Investment Performance Institute Inc., a firm that specializes in providing advanced-level practical capital markets training and consulting services to the financial services industry. Previously, he was a senior vice president of portfolio strategy and design for the national sales group at Prudential Securities Inc., and senior vice president of advanced training at PaineWebber Inc.

Over the last 30 years, Mr. Veale has trained more than 6,000 capital markets professionals on portfolio design, trading strategies, risk analysis, derivative pricing and strategies, fixed income portfolio management, equity pricing and analysis, CFA I and II Prep, and numerous other securities-related topics. He has published six books: *The Handbook of the U.S. Capital Markets* (Harper Business), *Bond Yield Analysis* (New York Institute of Finance), *Tapping the Small Business Market* (New York Institute of Finance), *Essential Investment Math* (International Financial Press), *Essential Asset Allocation* (International Financial Press), and *Stocks, Bonds, Options, Futures* (Prentice Hall Press). He has also published numerous financial articles in magazines, such as *Registered Representative*, *Cash Flow Magazine*, and *Medical Economics*.